The British Miniature

MRS. RAYMOND LISTER

Above by Joan Ayling; *Below* by Lisa de Montfort

These two miniatures represent the main trends—idealism and realism—
in contemporary miniature painting. Joan Ayling's idealistic miniature
contrasts strikingly with the almost stark realism of Lisa de Montfort's
interpretation of the same subject.

THE
BRITISH MINIATURE

By

RAYMOND LISTER, R.M.S., F.R.S.A.

Librarian of the Royal Society of Miniature Painters, Sculptors, and Gravers

LONDON
SIR ISAAC PITMAN & SONS, LTD.

FIRST PUBLISHED
1951

SIR ISAAC PITMAN & SONS, LTD.
PITMAN HOUSE, PARKER STREET, KINGSWAY, LONDON, W.C.2
THE PITMAN PRESS, BATH
PITMAN HOUSE, LITTLE COLLINS STREET, MELBOURNE
27 BECKETTS BUILDINGS, PRESIDENT STREET, JOHANNESBURG

ASSOCIATED COMPANIES
PITMAN PUBLISHING CORPORATION
2 WEST 45TH STREET, NEW YORK
SIR ISAAC PITMAN & SONS (CANADA), LTD.
(INCORPORATING THE COMMERCIAL TEXT BOOK COMPANY)
PITMAN HOUSE, 381–383 CHURCH STREET, TORONTO

MADE IN GREAT BRITAIN AT THE PITMAN PRESS, BATH
E1—(D.107)

TO
MY WIFE

PREFACE

IT is now some years since a general handbook was published on the British miniature—that beautiful and fascinating art which has flourished on our soil for well over a thousand years. It is true that in recent years much has been written on the subject of Nicholas Hilliard and his contemporaries, but great though these painters were they represented only one phase in a long and interesting development which began in Celtic monasteries at the dawn of Britain's civilized history, hundreds of years before Hilliard's birth. I have written this book partly in the hope that this true perspective may be restored, partly in the hope of meeting the demand for an up-to-date general handbook on the subject, and partly in the hope that such a book may help to assure the future of British miniature painting.

I should like to make grateful acknowledgment to all those who have courteously and patiently allowed me to examine specimens from their collections; to the British Museum, the Victoria and Albert Museum, the Syndics of the Fitzwilliam Museum, the Librarian of Trinity College, Dublin, the Dean of Lichfield, the Librarian of Trinity College, Cambridge, the National Maritime Museum, Greenwich, and to others for allowing works in their collections to be reproduced; to my friend, Mr. Arthur K. Astbury for his frank criticisms; and lastly to my wife, Pamela, for her patient co-operation and criticisms and for typing the manuscript.

RAYMOND LISTER

West Wratting
Cambridgeshire

CONTENTS

CONTENTS

LIST OF PLATES

IN THE TEXT

AT THE END OF THE TEXT
The Subject Miniature

LIST OF PLATES

The Portrait Miniature

LIST OF PLATES

The Contemporary School of Miniature Painters

The Silhouette

CHAPTER ONE

Introduction

FOR years the English have allowed to be blazoned around the world the fiction that they are an inartistic race. With sturdy English pride, and doubtless thinking of their football, their textiles, and other such materialistic matters, they themselves have boasted that they are too down to earth, too full of solid worth, and too essentially sensible to bother about such fantastic subjects as painting, music, and sculpture.

So far as the larger visual arts are concerned it is true that on the whole their achievements have not been outstanding; but their literature and their architecture are among the best in the world, and so are their water-colour and miniature painting, which are unsurpassed by any other nation in Europe.

There is at present real evidence of a new interest in the arts in general. Exhibitions of paintings, of sculpture, of objects of art and virtu, which before the Second World War would have been thought of limited appeal, now attract the attention of hundreds of thousands of people. It is in the hope that I may be able to introduce some of these people to an art so worthy of their interest, yet one so easily overlooked, that I have written this book on British miniature painting.

Miniatures are, indeed, easily passed by. In their size is both their chief charm and their chief disadvantage. Usually no more than a few square inches in size, it is not easy for them to compete with larger works of art for the attention of critics and art-historians. But the very fact that they have escaped attention in recent years gives them a special appeal to the individual art-lover and collector. They have no artificially inflated value, either financial or artistic, and they possess a type of intimacy that larger works lack.

THE DEFINITION OF A MINIATURE

Before going any further it will be as well to define the miniature. Generally speaking, to use an analogy, it is to larger painting what chamber music is to the symphony. One society of miniature painters has laid down that the miniature may be executed in any medium and upon any material. It must not measure more than seven inches by five inches, and must, of course, be in miniature style. Heads in portrait miniatures must not be more than two inches long.

So much for an official description of what a miniature should be. The layman, however, needs a little more explanation. It is obvious enough that not every picture that measures seven inches by five inches or less is a miniature, for there are enormous numbers of paintings with such measurements that do not come into the same category. Where then is the dividing line? It is to be found in the manner of execution—the miniature style referred to in the society's ruling just mentioned. This style can be anything from a diminutive impressionism to a highly polished photographic finish, but the brush strokes with which a miniature is painted should be small, in order that they may be proportionate to the size of the work. One may, for example, paint with a pointillist technique (placing dots of primary colours close to one another), but it would be wrong to use dots of the same size as those used by Seurat, the nineteenth-century French exponent of this style.

This, however, is merely a question of technique, and the smallness of the work needs some further justification. There is no point in painting a tiny work just for the sake of its small size, and such an approach may lead to bad art. A miniature is painted "in miniature" as a means to an end, because it achieves results which could not be obtained by other means. Its size can be justified on many grounds: by the ease with which it can be carried and the intimacy which naturally results, by its conditions of use, or by a particularly intense and gem-like appearance aimed at by the artist in portraying his subject. Illustrations for illuminated manuscripts or paintings for setting in rings, brooches, and other forms of jewellery must obviously be painted in miniature. And at the moment there is a special though temporary justification for its size, in the cramped living conditions in most of modern Europe. Few people to-day have space enough to collect, far less to display, large pictures; but a collection of miniatures can be housed in a cabinet, or displayed on the walls of a cottage. No better picture could be chosen for a small house or flat than the miniature, for in a room where a larger picture would be overpowering, the miniature, with its intimate charm, comes into its own.

ITS ART FORM AND HUMAN FUNCTION

So much for the miniature considered, so to speak, physically. What of it as an art form, and what is its human function?

The decorative nature of the miniature is quite distinct from that of the larger picture. It partakes, indeed, of the quality of a jewel. Its colours should sparkle like those of a gem and it should have the depth and richness of a ruby, or the starry lustre of a sapphire or a topaz. Dullness or muddiness should have no place in it.

If we examine the miniature against the background of painting as a whole, we realize that, alone amongst the visual arts, miniature painting has been uncontaminated by the more eccentric modern developments. Further, by its very nature, it demands good execution. It is so often held in the hand that clumsy or amateurish execution would soon be detected. Slipshod execution is much in evidence in some of the techniques used in the larger forms of painting to-day. Students wanting to take short cuts are often tempted to ape Picasso and Matisse, mistaking the considered distortions of these masters for something they certainly are not. Of course, not all modern tendencies in art are to be condemned, but it cannot be denied that some of the methods of the "moderns" make it easy for the amateur (or, worse, the *poseur*) to hide his shortcomings. No such evasions are open to the miniaturist, however, for the slightest clumsiness in his work becomes evident at once to the most casual observer.

The technique of many painters of large pictures might indeed improve if they occasionally submitted themselves to the discipline of this art. The miniature curbs eccentricity and disciplines, whilst at the same time keeping free, artistic development; and the miniaturist, avoiding extreme experimentalism, is also saved from the dead ends which indiscipline has produced in past centuries and will inevitably produce again.

It must be admitted that at the moment the miniature has little to offer the main stream of large painting apart from its moderating and disciplinary influences. In the past, however, it has made valuable technical and aesthetic contributions to that stream, and may well do so again. The miniature in illuminated manuscripts, for instance, long dominated styles in other forms of painting, and many problems of perspective and "atmosphere" were solved in such miniatures long before artists applied these discoveries to larger work. The Master of Mary of Burgundy, a Flemish book-painter of the fifteenth century, about whom nothing is known personally save this name, made experiments in *plein air* painting (the representation of atmosphere), the full effect of which on the mainstream of European painting was not observable for many years.

I have already suggested that the size of the miniature has a good deal to do with the scant attention it has received in recent years from art experts. Another reason lies in the fact that there was a break in the art's tradition caused by the invention of the photograph. At that time—the early part of the nineteenth century—the art of miniature painting seemed to be dying, or at best to be thenceforth a branch of art fit only for the antiquarian. It is only during the last fifty or sixty years that there has been any revival of interest. Now, however, miniaturists in this country are beginning to pick up the threads of a tradition which goes back to the dawn of culture in Britain.

The painter of miniatures, or limner as he was called in days gone by ("limner" is derived from the same root as "illuminator": he who "lights up" a manuscript), experiences a peculiar joy in his work. It is true that to work within such a small painting surface and to produce such a gem-like finish requires long experience and practice, but the necessarily long apprenticeship is amply justified by the satisfaction which comes to the developed artist. No one can deny that the painter of larger-sized pictures has his creative joys, but they are of a vastly different kind from those of the miniaturist. The artist who can create with his brush a starry jewel which for sheer brilliance rivals a fine diamond, experiences an emotional uplift which springs, not only from the delight in craftsmanship but also from the creation of a work that is primarily concerned with being pleasing and decorative.

Moreover, the miniature painter, like the collector of his work, can economize in space. He needs no special studio for his work. It is, in fact, better for him not to set apart a special room for his painting but to do it in the intimate surroundings of the sitting-room or drawing-room; his is an intimate art which should be produced in intimate surroundings. His equipment can be kept in a small writing-desk and put away out of sight in a few minutes. Yet from a Lilliputian collection of tools and colours he can produce a microcosm of his visual experiences as impressive as anything a painter of titanic canvases could hope to achieve, in spite of the magnitude of his labours.

The portrait miniature has important historical value. To look into the faces of such people as Queen Elizabeth, Oliver Cromwell, and George IV— to mention but three—as they are portrayed by the miniaturists of their times is to experience a thrill almost akin to that of meeting them in the flesh. Nobody can fail to be fascinated by an art that brings great personalities so vividly to life and enables one to enjoy their presence in one's own drawing room.

The subject miniature, too, has similar charms and to examine a collection of them is like holding up a diminishing-glass to the world's past.

The succeeding chapters of this book will amplify what has been said in the last few pages and should make it clear how alluring the miniature can be, not only to the collector, the artist, and the connoisseur, but also to the man in the street. It is one of the most charming forms of painting and it will repay with interest the attention devoted to it.

CHAPTER TWO

The Subject Miniature

MINIATURES fall broadly into two main classes, that of the portrait miniature and that of the subject miniature. Into the second of these two classes fall all miniatures that represent anything other than straightforward portraits.

EARLY FORMS OF THE SUBJECT MINIATURE

To a modern observer, the portrait miniature has been the most obvious and popular group for something like the last five hundred years. But in point of antiquity it must give first place to the subject miniature, for this originated so long ago that it is virtually impossible to give anything like a correct date, or even period, for its first appearance. Its place of origin, however, may be safely assumed to have been Egypt, for many papyri belonging to that country's remote history contain small pictures which are really miniatures. Specimens of such pictures are to be seen in the many Books of the Dead displayed in museums, and a glance will show what a close resemblance they have to much of the later miniature painting in illuminated manuscripts.

China and India, too, produced at an early date much work bearing a close relationship to miniature painting, and the traditions of these countries doubtless influenced our own at times, through the common meeting-place of East and West in the Arabian trading grounds, whence textiles were imported in the Middle Ages. These Oriental influences also reached the European schools of paintings by the indirect route through Byzantium, whose artists assimilated them before passing them on.

But whatever the remote origins of the art were, we do know that the miniature had its origins in those decorations in illuminated manuscripts which in the first place were little more than calligraphic flourishes in the margins. In fact the word "miniature" itself is derived from the name of the vermilion pigment, known as *minium*, with which these decorations were so often

PLATE I

13 × 9½ in.

THE BOOK OF KELLS
Trinity College, Dublin.

applied. From this the painter was sometimes referred to in Latin texts as *miniator*, and subsequently his pictures came to be called "miniatures." Originally miniatures were not necessarily small in size but, from the fact that being book-illustrations they were usually small, the word miniature came to be applied as a general term for any small-sized object. The root of this word, as will be seen from the foregoing, has nothing to do with the word "minute," which is an adaptation of the Latin *minutus*.

It is impossible to say with any degree of accuracy at what date illuminated books were first generally used in Europe, but they certainly existed in the later Roman Empire, and they may have been used in Ancient Greece, although there is no existing manuscript to support this. We have Pliny's authority that a large number of manuscripts of this kind existed in the first century before Christ.

THE CELTIC SCHOOL

Of the early contributions to the art of illuminating in the British Isles the most outstanding came from Ireland. The Irish monks, owing to their sheltered life on one of the most western islands of the continent, surrounded by a wide and inclement sea, enjoyed security from the ravages of those troubled times, and were able to develop their art of book-painting to a peak of technical refinement such as has never been seen before or since.

An interesting point in the appearance of this early work is its close relationship to the art of the goldsmith, for the patterns used in the decorations are often only goldsmith's designs transferred to the texture of paint. In fact it is certain that in some cases the same monk was responsible for both the decoration of the book itself, and for the gold and jewelled cover that enclosed it. The many interlacing lines, knots and spirals in the miniatures are obviously copies of the wired lines, known as *cloisons*, that played such a large part in the enamels produced by the monks as part of their jewelled work.

The Book of Durrow (Plate IX), now in Trinity College, Dublin, is probably the earliest Celtic manuscript extant, and certainly one of the earliest direct contributions to the tradition of British miniature painting. Its name is taken from that of the monastery where according to tradition it was created. It is difficult to decide how, and where, the style in which this manuscript is decorated originated, especially in view of the fact that the artist was obviously not experimenting, but working in a highly-developed style. In view of this it may be that there was a school of illuminators working in Ireland at an even earlier date; unfortunately there is no evidence of this, and we have no earlier manuscripts of a similar type. In his book on Anglo-Saxon art (see Bibliography) Mr. T. D. Kendrick puts forward the interesting theory that much of the interlacing scroll work was a local development of classical patterns on Roman tessellated pavements. Certainly, it seems strange that such a sudden development should take place, but many combinations of circumstances and influences may have been responsible for the style's origin, combinations which we are at a loss to unravel from this period in time. The Book of Durrow is signed by one Columba; some have sought to identify this personage with Saint Columba, famous as the founder of the monastery on the Isle of Iona. This is conjecture, but more evidence than we possess at present would be required in order to prove it with certainty.

The finest gem of this period is the wonderful Book of Kells (Plate I) which also reposes in Trinity College, Dublin. Produced in the eighth century, this book was for many years in the possession of Kells Cathedral Church, after which it is named. From the point of view of technique it is the most wonderful example of book painting that human hands have ever produced. One expert found over one hundred and fifty interlacements of lines in the space of one square inch, each one of which could be resolved into a soluble knot! Nobody with any knowledge of the technique of miniature painting could look at this remarkable work without a feeling of awe. Its rich colour and graceful linear designs combine to give an effect of opulence and majesty. The writer has known of experts, whose job it is to copy old works of this kind, who have broken down in despair after spending months on one page of this book. At few periods in the whole history of any art have technical mastery and clear artistic vision been so amazingly combined as they are in this work.

Irish monks crossed the sea to the west coast of Scotland, and established churches there centred round the Isle of Iona, where a monastery had been founded by St. Columba in the sixth century. It must, however, be remembered that, great as was the work done by the foundation of St. Columba, it was not the only connexion between Ireland and England at the time and that cultural influences came through other monasteries, such as that of Malmesbury, and through such Irish-trained ecclesiastics as Agilbercht, second bishop of Wessex.

A company of monks led by one named Aidan were summoned by King Oswald of Northumbria from Iona (where Oswald had earlier taken shelter in exile and received Christianity) to preach to the Northumbrians. They arrived in 634 and established a monastery on the Island of Lindisfarne, of which foundation Aidan, later to be canonized, became Bishop and Abbot. He died in 651. In the following century Lindisfarne Abbey developed into one of the chief centres for the production of illuminated manuscripts.

The illuminations produced on Lindisfarne (Plate X) are very similar in type to those of the Book of Kells, except that there are far more concessions to realism. Italian influences, brought by missionaries from the Roman Church, are to be seen, especially in the painting of the figures, where the calligraphic approach had weakened in favour of a more realistic, and more painterly, vision. The same dexterity is there, however, and the qualities that go to make the purely Irish work so remarkable are still in evidence.

In the ninth century the Vikings carried out many brutal plundering raids on this colony, and in the year 878, unable to resist such attacks any longer, those monks who were fortunate enough to have escaped annihilation sailed for the mainland, carrying with them the body of St. Cuthbert (who had been one of their number in years gone by) and a magnificent copy of the Gospels. After reaching the mainland they set sail for Ireland, only to run into a terrible storm, in which the book was washed overboard into the sea. The ship was driven back ashore, where the monks, at first downcast, found to their joy that the precious book had been washed up by the tide and was still comparatively unharmed. The book was placed in Cuthbert's coffin and buried with him at Durham Minster, which the fugitive monks founded after their unsuccessful attempt to sail for Ireland. In 1104 Cuthbert's body was exhumed, and the Gospels were once again sent to their original home on Lindisfarne, where a new monastery had been founded in 1093, on the site of the ruins of the former building. At the dissolution of the monasteries under Henry VIII, the Gospels had another narrow escape from injury, when their gold covers were stripped off to help fill that monarch's coffers. Luckily for posterity, the manuscript itself was left unharmed, and, after passing through many vicissitudes of ownership, is now housed in the British Museum.

This famous Book of the Gospels of St. Cuthbert was, in fact, created some time after that saint's death. Eadfrith, eighth bishop of Lindisfarne from 698 to 721, wrote it; his successor Aethelwold decorated it; whilst the reputedly magnificient decoration of the binding was the work of an anchorite named Billfrith.

THE ANGLO-CELTIC SCHOOL

In time the Irish School of book-painting combined with local influences in England, which in their turn were derived mainly from the Byzantine and Italian Schools, to form the basis of the Anglo-Celtic School. Such a combination has already been noted in the case of the Lindisfarne Gospels in which, moreover, gold leaf, never encountered in purely Celtic work, had been used, although on a very small scale. It is obvious that the monk Aethelwold must have seen examples of work produced under the direct influence of the eastern schools of illuminating in Europe.

A later example of the Celtic tradition is the Gospels of St. Chad (Plate XI) in Lichfield Cathedral, and although this work was doubtless produced after the Lindisfarne Gospels it is much more in the direct calligraphic tradition and reverts to the native style entirely. It makes no concessions whatsoever to the greater realism of the European work.

The main Irish tradition steadily degenerated after the heights reached by the monks of Lindisfarne, as is clearly illustrated both by the Gospels of Macdurnan, now in Lambeth Palace Library, and by the Book of Deer, in Cambridge University Library, the Book of Deer surely showing the lowest depths of degeneracy to which a once virile art can sink. The influence of the earlier work, on the other hand, had been spread far and wide, and manuscripts showing strong Irish influences were to be seen as far afield as Switzerland, Germany, and Italy.

The Byzantine and Italian influences in the Anglo-Celtic School were helped to gain their ascendancy by the growing power of the Roman Church, which had been introduced into England by St. Augustine, founder of the See of Canterbury. The indigenous Celtic Church was independent of Rome at that time, being ruled by the Abbot of Iona. After many conferences and discussions, St. Wilfrid of Ripon brought the north of England under the Church of Rome by an agreement reached at the Synod of Whitby in 664.

The chief artistic outcome of this amalgamation was to bring even stronger Eastern European influences to bear upon the native school of illuminating, and the Celtic style gradually decreased in importance, although many of its motifs long remained an integral part of English book painting. The ascendancy of the continental influence was furthered by such men as Benedict Biscop, who founded the monasteries of Wearmouth and Jarrow in the last quarter of the seventh century; this monk made many voyages to Rome and brought back examples of Italian art with him, in the form both of illuminations and of larger paintings. The result was that certain English monasteries were producing work in a continental manner, alongside others working in the native idiom. The most famous example of such a work now in existence is the Codex Amiatinus (now in the Laurentian Library, Florence) which was produced at the monastery at Jarrow, to the order of the first abbot, Ceolfrith, who took it with him on a journey to Rome, with the intention of presenting it to the Pope. His death en route, at Langres in 716, however, prevented this. A brilliant reproduction of the best continental writing, the Codex Amiatinus is one of the greatest of all uncial manuscripts.

The year 673 was an auspicious one for English book production, and for letters in general, for it saw the birth of Baeda, more familiarly known as the Venerable Bede. This truly great personality, who was one of the last men of learning to know the Greek and the Hebrew languages and the hypotheses of the great Greek philosophers, until the revival of interest in them at the time of the Renaissance, made the Abbey of Jarrow (where he died in 735) a great centre for beautifully illuminated manuscripts. Owing to his efforts the Benedictine Abbey of Durham was raised to a position of international artistic eminence. The eighth century was, in fact, a period during which the English School of miniature painting became the most highly developed of its kind in Europe; this eventful century saw the birth of a true English School, which welded together the Celtic and European influences into a cohesive whole. In addition to the abbeys already mentioned, York and Winchester took an active part in these developments. For many years after this time, England was without doubt the world's most out-standing producer of illuminated manuscripts, as well as being the guardian of the great classical traditions of Europe which for so long were prevented from flourishing by the wars that ravaged the whole of the continent. England, being an island, was isolated from the main impact of these upheavals, and classicism might have faded away altogether but for this geographical asset.

On the continent peace came with the victories of Charles the Great, who in 768 became King of the Franks and in 800 Emperor of the West. This monarch was a great patron of the arts and his reign witnessed a great revival of the art of illumination throughout his dominions. This was largely the result of the work of Alcuin, one time Dean of York, who had been sent by Offa, King of Mercia, as an envoy to Charles towards the end of the eighth century. Alcuin became Abbot of the Benedictine monastery of St. Martin at Tours, and as he brought with him the influence of the brilliant British School of illuminating, the Carolingian School (which, of course, is named after the emperor himself) developed into the Anglo-Carolingian School. At about the same time decorative influences from Arabia, brought to the West in the form of textiles and various domestic furnishings, made their presence felt. Many beautiful forms were evolved from these combinations.

THE ANGLO-SAXON SCHOOL

Whilst these developments were taking place on the continent, England was suffering from her share of pagan vandalism, being ravaged by various Danish invasions which were accompanied by looting, arson, and bloodshed. This resulted in the development of the purely English style of illuminating being brought to a complete standstill. King Alfred, however, at last brought about a state of comparative peace in his war-weary land, and the arts were once again allowed to take their rightful place in the nation's life.

Remembering the impression that had been made upon him by Charles the Great's magnificent library at Aix-la-Chapelle, which he had visited whilst on his journey to Rome as a boy, Alfred sent monks to the continent for instruction in the art of book-production, so that similar treasures might once again be produced in his own land. These monks brought back our main traditions, which had been firmly planted there by Alcuin and had then been enriched by the influences mentioned above.

Alfred himself was indeed a great monarch, and combined in his person the qualities of a just ruler, a fine soldier, and an enthusiastic patron of learning and the arts. His patronage of the arts is amply attested to by the numerous scriptorii or writing-rooms which were founded under his influence in the various Benedictine monasteries, an especial case being that of Winchester. A scriptorium, existing at Winchester Abbey before the reign of Alfred, was said to have been founded by St. Swithun, who became bishop of the See, and this may well have provided an example for the King; but his greatest incentive must surely have come from what he had seen in his youthful visit to the continent. In any case, the fact remains that Alfred founded a second abbey at Winchester, with another scriptorium, the Abbeys coming to be known as the Old and New Minster, respectively. We are lucky in that we know the name of one accomplished individual artist working at the Old Minster, called Godeman, who was responsible for much fine work.

By the efforts of Alfred and his monks the Anglo-Saxon school of illuminating was developed, and in the tenth century, by virtue of the work that was executed at Winchester, England once more became the producer of the finest illuminated manuscripts in Europe. Much of the work produced elsewhere in this country was very poor, however, and was not to be compared with the great examples emanating from Winchester itself.

THE ANGLO-NORMAN SCHOOL

The eleventh century saw a gradual general improvement, but the Anglo-Saxon School was eliminated with the coming of William of Normandy in 1066, and from this time England and Normandy, united under one monarch, became the fertile soil from which sprang the Anglo-Norman School of illuminating.

It cannot be denied that the Norman conquerors took the artistic lead for some time after the Conquest, for most of the heads of the great church establishments were of Norman blood and their powers were far-reaching. At the same time, it was a period of great native artistic development, and incidentally one that saw a greater measure of realism introduced into miniatures than had ever been known before. For the first time, gold embellishments were used on a wide and lavish scale.

The Crusades, which followed soon after the Conquest, were responsible for once again bringing many near-Eastern influences to bear upon the art. Men's minds, too, were becoming more free and the influence of the social revolution which took place in France at the end of the eleventh century was felt throughout Europe, causing the older and long-accepted Christian classicism to give way to a more liberal outlook. In time, such combined influences gave birth to what is known as Gothic art, an aesthetic movement that swept over most of the continent, causing a sensitive linear conception to take the place of the more monumental and classical Byzantine and Romanesque growths. The new art was more free, more poetic, and for the first time in its history miniature painting ceased to be either classic or barbaric. It came out into the open air, contacted Nature, and became romantic.

The Normans were certainly hard task-masters to the conquered Anglo-Saxons, but whatever else they may have done, they undoubtedly enabled the art of our island to be carried to greater heights than it had reached for some time. This upward growth reached its peak during the thirteenth century, when the true Anglo-Norman style of miniature painting came into full flower. At this time England assumed leadership in the principal fine arts over the whole of the known western world. All this was accomplished despite the unpropitious circumstances existing at the beginning of the thirteenth century, which were largely the result of the misrule of King John and of his actions against the clergy. But during the reign of Henry III, which lasted from 1216 until 1272, almost unbelievable progress was made; whatever faults he had—and they were certainly many—this King was one of the most lavish of all the patrons of the arts in our history. Even in Italy, where achievement in the fine arts was to be carried to such glorious heights at the time of the Renaissance, there was nothing to show that could compare with the English work produced during the reigns of Henry III and Edward I.

One of the dominant artistic personalities of the thirteenth century was Matthew Paris, historian and monk of St. Albans. In the second quarter of the century this artist assumes a position of great importance in the development of British miniature painting; his work, mostly carried out in a wash-and-line technique, is of outstanding skill and interest, and possesses great

PLATE II

Ele sime aungele sona sa busine. e io or une uois
del corneis del corn auter ki est deuaunt les oiz
de deu disaunt al sist aungre ki auerr la busine. Desliez
les qtre aungeles ki sunt liez en le grauntt sluue de
eufraur. E qtre aungeles sunt desliez. ki estetent apa-
rillez. en hourt. e en iur. e en meis. e en an. ke il tuaser
la rere parue des houmes. e le numbre del host a che
ual. umr sei. mil ser dis mil. e io or le numbre de eus.

Par le sime aungel sur signiszel les martirs. P le corn auter se
puite eglise est entendu. P les qtre conuerí. les qtre euangelise
S enr iohan oi une uois. des qtre corneis. pur ro ke une tei e une
aprise ek la quele. les qtre liuers del euangile enseignont. P les q-
tre aungeles sur endui qtre reaumes. Le regne des asstriens. e des
psauns. e des grezeis. e des romauns. P eufraure est entendu cest
munde. P les liens des qtre aungeles sur entendus les paroles
de nostre seignur. kar ro ke il sust par sa pouste. i eo est il dir auerr co
maun
de.

17 × 12 in.

SCENES FROM THE APOCALYPSE
Trinity College Library,
Cambridge, MS. R 16.2 f.10 R.

poetic insight. Probable examples of his work, or at least of work carried out under his direction, are in the Historia Anglorum (British Museum) and the Chronica Majora (Corpus Christi College, Cambridge).

Amongst other English illuminators of those days were members of a family named Fitz-Otho, various members of which, apart from being illuminators, were goldsmiths and makers of dies for coins. The magnificent golden shrine of Edward the Confessor was the work of this family.

The Abbeys of St. Albans, Westminster, and Winchester were among the most notable producers of illuminations during the thirteenth century, and were responsible for some of the finest illuminations that the world has ever known.

LATER ENGLISH ILLUMINATED MANUSCRIPTS

After the end of the thirteenth century the quality of English art declined and it was no longer comparable with the great period it had just been through. This is mainly attributable to the Wars of the Roses and to the Black Death, whose disrupting effects hampered artistic achievement. Notwithstanding, much excellent work was done, particularly in the abbeys of East Anglia and of York, Winchester, St. Albans, and Canterbury (Plate XII).

During this period richly decorated psalters were in increasing demand for the laity as well as for the clergy, which provided an opportunity for the introduction, on a wider scale than had hitherto been seen, of historiated initials—that is, initials containing miniatures illustrating events and persons referred to in the text. Other popular types of manuscript were the large Bibles (often occupying several volumes), and the Bestiaries, which were moralizing natural histories consisting of simple allegories such as the representation of the Devil as a crafty fox and of Christ at His Resurrection as a phoenix. Most magnificent of all were the Apocalypses, produced from the middle of the thirteenth century up to the end of the first quarter of the fourteenth century. There is a particularly fine example in the library of Trinity College, Cambridge (Plate II).

At this period there appeared the first obvious developments towards the creation of the art of the portrait miniature, for the initial letters were often made to contain medallions with various figures, heraldic charges, and imaginative portraits of kings and prophets from the Old Testament. The most important decorative scheme in the psalter was to be found on the Beatus page, which takes its name from the opening words of the first psalm, "Beatus vir." The letter B was usually elaborated into a system of interlacing decorations, grotesque figures, and miniatures. The favourite subject for such capital letters was a representation of the Tree of Jesse.

The revival of the art of illuminating which followed the end of the Black Death showed a complete change in style, for which foreign influences were largely responsible; such influences were encouraged by Richard II's two marriages to foreign princesses, Anne of Bohemia and Isabella of France. Notwithstanding the break in activity between 1360 and 1400, some manuscripts of great beauty were produced, thus keeping alive the central tradition of the English School.

The remarkable illuminations produced during the fourteenth century owed much of their splendour to the fact that the order of monks producing the largest quantity, that of St. Benedict, was an international organization, its members thus being enabled to form an eclectic school, built up by frequent migration of members of the order from one country to another. The result of all this was a truly international art and an almost uniform style of illuminating throughout most of western Europe; in many cases it is almost impossible to decide whether a manuscript was produced in England or on the continent. This international exchange was not restricted to clerical artists, for growing numbers of lay artists, who formed themselves into guilds, also travelled from country to country. We know, for instance, that English miniature painters were working in Paris early in the fourteenth century.

The same century saw great activity by the East Anglian monasteries, led by Bury St. Edmunds, Ely, Norwich, Peterborough, and Ramsey. These were, more than any other group, responsible for the brilliance of this period of the art.

The fifteenth century showed a deterioration in the style of manuscripts produced in this country, and although many examples were technically brilliant, there is no doubt that the art was declining. It had not travelled far in this direction, however, before the rudimentary portrait miniature, in the form in which it became so popular in the sixteenth century, had begun to take shape; for the many little portraits and medallions in the borders of the illuminations, which had formerly been purely imaginative, began to be replaced with true portraits of reigning monarchs, monks, and court and church dignitaries.

The first part of the fifteenth century saw the creation of the Psalter and Hours of John, Duke of Bedford, which is now in the British Museum, where it has been since 1929 (Plate XVII). Largely the work of an artist named Herman, this work contains many portrait heads of the type just mentioned, most of which are obviously painted from life.

On the continent the centre of book-painting had shifted to Flanders, and the Flemish influence is apparent in many English manuscripts of the fifteenth century. The decline in the French influence in England may be attributed in part to the facts that England had lost all her French possessions except Calais during the hundred years' war and that France, exhausted after the struggle, was concerned with putting her own house in order. On the other hand one must not overlook the still brilliant, though decadent, French group, headed by Jean Fouquet (c. 1420–1480), a contemporary of the poet François Villon and one of the most brilliant book-painters of the century. But Flanders had definitely become the hub of the miniaturist's activity and her influence would have been felt here even had contact with France been easier.

Illumination received its death-blow in this country from the introduction of printing in 1477, and although it survived for a time, and even at the present day is used for ceremonial purposes, by its very nature it could not rival the new craft either in cheapness of production or in availability, and consequently it ceased to exist as a truly functional art. For a time the illuminator's services were used for the enrichment of printed books, but this practice had an even shorter life here than it did on the continent, for Caxton used woodcut initials for his capitals whilst continental printers still employed illuminators to paint them.

From this time onwards the subject miniature waned in popularity, and the book-painter's art was transformed into that of the illustrator. Artists like Albrecht Dürer, who might easily have been miniaturists in earlier times, looked to the woodcut and the etching for their means of expression and founded a new tradition for this particular function of the subject miniature, the true representatives of which in our own time are artists like Edmund Dulac and Agnes Miller Parker.

PETER OLIVER

Removed from its accustomed place within the book, the subject miniature appeared at first to be in a sorry plight, but before long other uses were found for it, although it must be admitted that its great days were at an end.

After the Reformation English subject-miniature painting was blessed with an artist of the first rank, in the person of Peter Oliver, the son of Isaac Oliver the great portrait miniaturist. Peter Oliver turned the miniature to another good and useful purpose, by making tiny copies of large pictures. Edward Norgate, the herald-miniaturist, wrote: "Histories in Lymning are strangers in England till of late years it pleased a most excellent King to command the Copieing of some of his owne pieces, of Titian, to be translated into English Lymning, which were indeed admirably performed by his Servant, Mr. Peter Oliver." This king, of course, was Charles I. One such copy is to be seen in the Jones Collection in the Victoria and Albert Museum (Plate III). It is a copy of a lost painting by Titian, "The Flight into Egypt," is painted on vellum, and measures six inches by nine and nine-sixteenth inches; it was executed in 1628. According to Vanderdoort's Catalogue of Charles I's Collection (compiled *circa* 1639) the original picture measured two feet eleven inches by five feet six inches.

The copying of large pictures in miniature enabled possessors of paintings to carry reminders of their favourite works with them on their travels, as well as being invaluable for recording purposes at a time when photography had yet to be invented. The example of the miniature just mentioned shows the value of these small copies, for without it we should know nothing of Titian's picture beyond verbal descriptions, inadequate and often misleading.

In this work, Oliver has succeeded in transferring the image of a Titian oil painting of about fifteen square feet to a surface of less than sixty square inches. This, in itself, is no mean feat, but Oliver has left us the measure of his greatness in that he has also rendered in the minor scale all the aesthetic qualities of a Titian. Admittedly, it is difficult to say how far he has succeeded in keeping to the spirit of the original when the latter no longer exists, but we know enough of Titian's other work to form a fair estimate of Oliver's achievement. Oliver, in this work, accomplished one of the most difficult tasks that a miniature painter can set himself, for he took a work by another

PLATE III

$6 \times 9\frac{9}{16}$ in.

PETER OLIVER
The Flight into Egypt (After Titian)
Victoria & Albert Museum,
Jones Collection, No. 618.
Crown copyright.

great painter and recreated it in his own medium, without producing a pastiche or a plagiarism. This is a feat that few have completely succeeded in achieving, and in this facet of miniature painting Peter Oliver is almost without an equal and certainly without a superior.

Peter Oliver was born at some date between the years 1594 and 1601. He died in 1647 and was buried at Blackfriars on 22 December of that year. Beyond these facts we know little of him—a sparseness of information that is but too often repeated in the case of so many other miniaturists.

With Oliver a completely new development in miniature painting is apparent, in that larger painting begins to exercise a definite influence on the art. Hitherto its influence had been but small, and, in fact, until quite late in the Middle Ages it had been the miniature that had completely dominated the style of large painting. The altar-pieces, wall-paintings, and panels that constituted almost the complete output of painters of large pictures in the Middle Ages were, almost without exception, painted on the lines of large miniatures. From now onwards larger painting, which had made such strides and risen to such sublime eminence at the Renaissance, especially on the continent, was to have an increasing influence on miniature painting. It is obvious that a miniaturist, set to copy their work, could not fail to come under the influence of the aesthetics and techniques of artists like Correggio and Titian, even when their re-creations of their works were as successful as those of an artist of the stature of Peter Oliver.

The popularity of miniature copies increased, and, in this country at any rate, they account for the greater part of the subsequent history of the subject miniature up to the end of the eighteenth century. The painter of subject miniatures was to find this path his most lucrative, but, with the exception of a few individual artists, the art became merely a reflection of large painting so that in such cases the history of one becomes the history of the other. The exceptions were notable, however, and beginning with Peter Oliver, we have quite a number in the history of our art of whom we can be justly proud.

LATER BRITISH SUBJECT MINIATURISTS

After Peter Oliver the most considerable figure in British subject-miniature painting was Bernard Lens. This artist will be mentioned again in the chapter on portrait miniatures, but his work as a subject miniaturist is no less important. His fine "Landscape with River and Figures" (Plate XIX) executed in gouache on vellum, shows what a considerable copyist he was. Taken from an oil painting by John Vandervaart, the work is a fine example of minute and intricate organization. Although it is but a small painting, measuring ten and a quarter inches by seven and thirteen-sixteenth inches, the artist has managed to suggest spaciousness and depth to a remarkable degree. Some of the credit for this must, of course, be accorded to Vandervaart, creator of the original, but as in the case of Oliver's copy of the Titian, credit must also go to the miniaturist for having made the transfer a creative entity and for having avoided the pitfall of mere copying.

To James Scouler goes the credit of having been the first artist to show miniatures at the Royal Academy. Up to 1787, in which year he probably died, he had had over thirty such works accepted. His miniature of the goddess Diana (Plate XXIV) may in the opinion of some come under the heading of the portrait miniature, but it really belongs to the subject group. It is a competently painted work, and, although somewhat sentimentalized, is most pleasing. It differs from the works just mentioned inasmuch as it is a completely imaginative miniature, and is in no way dependent upon an already existing painting for its conception.

The eighteenth century saw a movement towards imaginative subject miniatures like "Diana." One of the most prolific painters of these works was Samuel Shelley, who delighted in such mythological titles as "Love's complaint to Time," and "Nymphs feeding Pegasus," and also in scenes from Shakespeare. He was one of the founders of the Watercolour Society in 1805, and it was in his house that its formation was discussed. Shelley was born at Whitechapel during the middle period of the eighteenth century, and died in London in 1808. Although he had little training in painting, he was a fine colourist and produced some excellent work. In common with many other painters of the period he was greatly influenced by Sir Joshua Reynolds, and owed much of his style to that of the Academy's first president.

William Birch painted some pretty little enamel subject miniatures at about the same period as that in which Samuel Shelley was working. Although he emigrated to Philadelphia, he really belongs to the English School of miniature painters. He exhibited at the Royal Academy for about twenty years, beginning in 1775, and showed over forty works there. In some of his work he exemplifies the eroticism so common among French miniaturists of the period immediately preceding him, as in his "Landscape with Women Bathing" (Plate XVIII). Miniatures, on account of their intimacy and portability, lend themselves excellently to the rendering of erotic subjects. Fitted into the lids of snuff-boxes, or in many similar places, they filled in their day the same functions as the "pin-up" of our own, but with a great deal more taste. The landscape just mentioned is not so blatantly erotic as many French works, but the attitudes of the women, and their general presentation, are in direct contrast to the more romantic representation in Lens's noble work.

In the sphere of copies, the enamels of William Essex show competence and quality. From a technical point of view, the magnificent *trompe-l'œil* copy of a flower painting by Veerendael (Plate XX) would be difficult to surpass, although it somehow fails to be more than a technical *tour-de-force*. Of better quality artistically is his copy of William Hilton's "Cupid Disarmed by a Nymph" (Plate XXI).

William Essex was born in 1784, and died at Brighton in 1869. He was popular in his day both as a painter of animals and as an enamellist; and in 1839 he was appointed enamel-painter to Queen Victoria, a post that he thoroughly deserved, for, although his work did not approach that of the earlier miniaturists at their best, it was better than that of most of his contemporaries. Certainly better than that of Alfred Tidey (1808-1892), whose "White Mice" (Plate XXIII), apart from its display of technical skill, is a repulsive piece of sentimental homosexuality. The far-away look in the boy's limpid eyes, the rolled-up trouser leg, showing his calf, and the shirt carefully arranged to show his bared chest and shoulder are bad enough in themselves, but we are further inflicted with an ample Victorian pillar in the background and, of all things, the beggar-boy has washed! Compare him with Peter Paul Lens's portrait of a beggar-boy (Plate XXII), mentioned in the next chapter, and the difference between a real street arab and a bizarre day-dream is immediately apparent. So far had we travelled from the great days of the Lindisfarne Gospels that our artists could produce nothing better than this. But a thousand years is a long time for human achievement to remain at a consistently high level, and Alfred Tidey and his contemporaries at least helped to keep the art alive.

Other Victorian painters who produced subject miniatures, but who worked mainly in other directions, included Sir Edward Burne-Jones, who co-operated with William Morris to produce an illuminated manuscript of the Rubaiyat of Omar Khayyam, Millais, whose "Bridesmaid" is in the Fitzwilliam Museum at Cambridge, and Lord Leighton.

Apart from the work of one or two artists like Peter Oliver and Bernard Lens, the more recent history of the subject miniature, until the revival in this century, can show nothing to compare with those in many illuminated manuscripts of the Middle Ages. Our truly great achievements, after the fifteenth century, are to be found in the history of the portrait miniature, which is the subject of the next chapter.

CHAPTER THREE

The Portrait Miniature

LEGEND has it that the portrait miniature, as we know it to-day, was invented at the time of the French King Charles VIII's expedition to the Alps towards the end of the fifteenth century. It is said that the knights who went with him left their portraits in little with their loved ones, who in turn gave their likenesses to the men who were leaving to join the expedition. Whether this charming story is true or not, there is no doubt that ever since that period the portrait miniature has been the art's most popular form. There is nothing more intimate and pleasing than a good portrait miniature; nothing recalls so vividly the very presence of the person it represents. Little wonder that men in the past carried miniatures of their loved ones close to their hearts.

The portrait miniature, as we have seen in the preceding chapter, first made its appearance in illuminated manuscripts and was brought very near to perfection in the Bedford Psalter and Hours (Plate XVII). Who the genius was who first alighted on the idea of putting these little portraits in lockets we shall perhaps never know, but genius he was and we owe him a great debt for introducing to the world a charming form of art that has given pleasure to many generations.

HANS HOLBEIN THE YOUNGER

The first great portrait miniaturist in the history of the art was that many-sided genius, Hans Holbein the Younger. There had doubtless been artists before him who produced this type of work, but it was Holbein who really laid the firm foundations of miniature portrait painting and gave the English tradition its first great impetus.

Hans Holbein the Younger was born at the end of the fifteenth century at Augsburg, and followed in the profession of his father, who was also an artist. Through Erasmus, he was introduced to Sir Thomas More who took him into his service. But King Henry VIII heard of the artist's reputation and soon engaged him as his court painter. It has been said that after coming to London Holbein learned to paint miniatures from one Master Lucas, of whom nothing is known. Others say that he studied the art under Geraert Lucas Horembout, the Flemish book-painter, but this again is conjectural.

Holbein arrived in England in 1526 and lived here almost continuously until he died in 1543. He was a favourite at court, and his portraits of Henry and his courtiers provide an incomparable record of the period. Few other court artists have taken such good advantage of the opportunities presented by the colourful costume of his subjects, and few others penetrated so far as he did beyond this decoration, to plumb the depths of their characters. It is not surprising that such outstandingly good work was widely imitated, and for that reason it has always been difficult to authenticate with any degree of certainty; the examples which can be attributed to him beyond doubt are few.

At least one of his portraits had far-reaching results and the story which is told of it makes one wonder if Holbein made many concessions to beauty at the expense of veracity. The king wished to marry a Protestant princess after Jane Seymour's death, and Holbein was detailed to paint a portrait of Anne of Cleves, who was under consideration for his suit. Holbein greatly flattered that ill-favoured woman, with the result that Henry found but a "Flanders Mare" in the place of what he had been led to expect. For his part in the affair Thomas Cromwell, the king's chancellor, was executed, but Holbein was apparently unmolested. A miniature by Holbein of this Princess is in the Salting Collection at the Victoria and Albert Museum (Plate XXV), and the portrait which caused all the trouble is in the Louvre.

NICHOLAS HILLIARD

The first native English miniaturist to achieve greatness was Nicholas Hilliard, who founded his style on Holbein's, adapting it to the greater flamboyance of the Elizabethan age. There is some doubt about the exact date of Hilliard's birth, but it is now generally accepted as *c.* 1547. His father, Richard, was an Exeter goldsmith and his mother was a goldsmith's daughter. Nicholas himself was apprenticed to that trade and became a member of the Goldsmiths' Company. This training influenced his miniature painting considerably, for he always showed a jeweller's approach in his decorative conceptions and even set real gems into his painted work, greatly increasing its effect thereby. It is surely no mere coincidence that two of the greatest periods in the art of miniature painting were influenced by the jeweller's approach—the time of the Celtic illuminators who produced the magnificent Book of Kells, and the time of the Elizabethan portrait miniaturist, Nicholas Hilliard.

Nicholas was married twice, first to Alice Brandon, daughter of London's City Chamberlain, and second to a woman of whom nothing is known. It is thought that Alice bore him his son Laurence, who also became a miniature painter.

It is not known at what exact date Nicholas Hilliard was appointed goldsmith and limner to Queen Elizabeth, but it must have been somewhere in the late fifteen-sixties, for his first miniature of her belongs to that time. This portrait of the queen in state robes, now in the collection of the Duke of Portland, is certainly of great decorative value, but gives but little indication of what he was to achieve later. He was well paid for his services at Court, for there are records of many payments to him of what were for those days very large sums; and he was evidently popular, for he conversed freely with many eminent courtiers and even with the Queen herself. Later, however, he was in financial difficulties, for there exist various letters in which he appealed to Sir Robert Cecil, Earl of Salisbury and Lord High Treasurer of England, to use his influence to obtain assistance for him. When James I ascended the throne he also bestowed his patronage upon Hilliard, which he enjoyed until his death in 1619.

Even if Hilliard had not left behind him such a galaxy of exquisite miniatures, his place in the history of the art would have been assured by his important *Treatise Concerning the Arte of Limning*, which he wrote at the request of Richard Haydocke. This treatise, the oldest known manuscript of which is in the possession of the University of Edinburgh, is the most important document in the art's bibliography. It sets out, from the very beginning of its history, the aims, tenets, and technique of miniature portraiture. Every student and collector should make a point of reading it.

More will be said of this book in later chapters, but its historic importance must be emphasized. On the very first page the great limner has left us a colourful account of the miniature's functions: ". . . and yet it excelleth all other painting whatsoeuer in sondry points, in giuing the true lustur to pearle and precious stone, and worketh the metals gold or siluer with them-selfes, which so enricheth and innobleth the worke that it seemeth to be the thinge itse[l]fe, euen the worke of God and not of man, benning fittest for the decking of princes bookes or to put in jeuuells of gould and for the imitat[ion] of the purest flowers and most beautifull creaturs in the finest and purest coullers which are chargable, and is for the seruice of noble persons very meet in small voloms in privat maner for theem to haue the portraits and pictures of themselues, their peers, or any other. . . ." Whole books could hardly describe better the art's essential character.

Hilliard's miniatures were, like those of Holbein, still very closely related to the portraits in illuminated manuscripts. They were still based largely on the calligraphic tradition, being founded on a technique of line and pure colour, with the smallest degree of modelling that could be reconciled with the degree of realism he set out to obtain. The written descriptions of his sitters and their ages, too, were obviously a relic of the times when calligraphy and decoration were so closely entwined by the book-painters of the Middle Ages. Hilliard's work had great lyrical quality and could rise to really sublime heights as in the "Youth Leaning against a Tree among Roses" (Plate XXVIII). This wonderful miniature, in the Salting Collection, sums up that aspect of the Elizabethan age so well expressed, in other arts, by its sonnets and madrigals. It conveys to us, more than any large picture of its time, the romantic yearnings of its poets. And how could any larger picture hope to capture that feeling like the intimate miniature? This delightful work is the most suitable illustration that could be chosen for Shakespeare's sonnets themselves.

Yet another aspect of the Elizabethan age is portrayed in his portrait of an unknown man (Plate XXVI). This shows us another young dandy of the time, but of a different kind, for this is the type one would have expected to find on the stage at the Globe Theatre, delighting in the hoodwinking of Malvolio and in the pranks of Sir Toby Belch and Sir Andrew Aguecheek.

The adventurous spirit of the period was, of course, not neglected by Hilliard. Indeed how could it be by any patriotic Englishman when Sir Francis Drake and Sir Philip Sidney were in their prime? Perhaps better than anywhere else it is summed up in his portrait of George Clifford, third

Earl of Cumberland, as Queen's Champion (Plate XXVII). All the buccaneering swagger of the English adventurers of the period seem to be portrayed in these few square inches.

And among all these aspects of the Elizabethan age there shine brilliantly his numerous representations of the Queen herself, in many varieties of costume (Plate XXVI). Here surrounded by a majesty of state robes, there decked in ruff and jewels of almost unbelievable magnificence; here again in a simpler jewelled coronet and necklace; but always resplendent as the sun of her age and the artist's greatest inspiration.

Laurence Hilliard followed in his father's footsteps and produced some quite charming work; but he was working at a disadvantage, for his father had said almost all that the medium could be made to say about the Elizabethan age. Moreover, Laurence's miniatures are marred by a certain hardness and an almost complete lack of that lyrical quality so noteworthy in his father's work (Plate XXX).

ISAAC OLIVER

Hilliard's true artistic successor was his pupil, Isaac Oliver, who carried his master's style a stage further in the direction of complete realism. Whether such a step was for the good of the art or not is beside the point. It merely represents another way of looking at the same subject. Many people have sought to praise Oliver at the expense of Hilliard—even an authority of the stature of Dr. G. C. Williamson was guilty of this—but such comparisons are undesirable, for in art there are many ways of being right. In any case, both Hilliard and Oliver made valuable contributions to the art's development.

Compared with our knowledge of Hilliard's life, the facts about Isaac Oliver's are very sparse indeed. The varying dates given for the year of his birth range roughly from 1555 to 1568. We do know, however, that he was a pupil of Hilliard and that towards the end of the sixteenth century he was a finished artist. He was of Huguenot descent and was brought here by his parents to escape persecution in the land of his birth. Like Hilliard, he was the son of a goldsmith. Isaac married three times, his second wife being Sara Gheeraerts, who may have been a daughter of the artist, Marc Gheeraerts, who lived part of his life in England. He was naturalized in 1606, and is described in the official entry as "Isaack Olyver born at Rouen under the allyiance of the King of France." His death occurred in 1617, two years before that of his master. He left instructions in his will that "All my drawings already finished and unfinished and limned pictures, be they histories, stories, or anything of limning whatsoever, of my own hand work to my dearest son, Peter, if he shall live and exercise that art or science which he and I now do."

As we have said, Oliver strove towards a greater representation of realism than did his predecessor. Hilliard used no shadow in his work and thus arrived at a somewhat flat effect; Oliver on the other hand made use of it, and thus introduced an atmosphere of drama into his work, which had hitherto been absent from all miniature painting. From this alone it will be seen that his portraits are vastly different in aim from his master's. Hilliard's path led towards idealism, Oliver's towards realism. These two great artists considered together are complementary; and standing as they do at the awakening period of the portrait miniature's development, they formed an invaluable foundation that made possible all that was to follow.

Isaac Oliver's work was certainly not wanting in decorative value. His miniatures of a lady in masque costume, in the Victoria and Albert Museum, and of Henry Frederick Prince of Wales (both Plate XXX), in the Fitzwilliam Museum, Cambridge, are veritable riots of colour—a sure indication of the miniaturist's French origin. The placing of the heads in the space of the miniatures adds to their decorative effect. But the close relationship to illuminations is already disappearing and for his decorative effects Oliver concentrates upon realistic representations of his sitters and their clothes. Except in a few instances, fancy has given place to skill in reproduction and arrangement. The romantic Englishman has been followed by the realistic Frenchman.

Oliver was particularly outstanding in his larger miniatures. The famous portrait of a youth, supposed to represent Sir Philip Sidney, which is in the collection of H.M. the King at Windsor Castle and which is reproduced (Plate XXIX) by gracious permission of His Majesty, is a case in point. This takes us into the quiet and ordered garden of an Elizabethan mansion. The youth, sitting on a bank beneath a tree, looks enigmatically towards the viewer, whilst ordered flower-beds, an arcade, and a mansion fill the background. This work is nearer in spirit to the fifteenth-century illuminations than any other of Oliver's work. It might easily be an Anglicized version of a miniature taken from one of Fouquet's illuminations. In it the artist has successfully welded together the portrait and subject miniature to meet his demands. It is a triumph of conscious composition. Another larger miniature worthy of note is Oliver's full-length portrait of Richard Sackville, third Earl of Dorset (Plate XXXI). This is much more realistic than the one just mentioned, and much more typical of the artist. The nobleman's clothes, his face, and the furnishings of the room, right down to the rush matting, are all faithfully reproduced, and the whole gives an illusion of depth rarely encountered in such works at that time.

Oliver's insistence on a greater degree of realism does not mean that he was without imagination. Only an artist of great imaginative powers could have painted the delicate miniature of Lucy Harington, Countess of Bedford (Plate XXXII). This work, in spite of the fact that it is executed almost completely in black and white, glows with atmosphere and character. The shaded background has been used to great advantage to achieve the atmosphere, whilst the subtle rendering of the subject's face puts this amongst Oliver's finest work. Nor is it lacking in decorative value; the rendering of the embroidery on the dress is a clever adaptation of the decorative *motifs* from illuminated borders—yet another of Oliver's rare betrayals of his art's origins—and secures its effect magnificently. Without doubt Isaac Oliver made many valuable contributions to miniature painting.

PETER OLIVER

His son, Peter, has already been mentioned for his subject miniatures, but he also executed some excellent portrait miniatures (Plate XXXIII); in fact it is not easy to say whether father or son was the greater artist. Except where they are signed, it is extremely difficult and sometimes impossible to distinguish their work. Peter's work is, if anything, rather more lyrical than that of Isaac, but on the whole much the same characteristics are to be found in both.

Walpole related a romantic story about some of Peter Oliver's works. It appears that after the execution of Charles I the monarch's collection of miniatures was dispersed by the Commonwealth, and that Peter Oliver's widow, then living at Isleworth, had bought some of her husband's work.

When Charles II came to the throne he heard of this and, wishing to acquire the miniatures again, went in disguise to see Mrs. Oliver, who allowed him to see them. Upon being asked if she would sell them, she replied that she was keeping them in case the King should wish to have them. When he heard this Charles immediately made himself known to her, and she allowed him to take the miniatures away with him. He later sent a messenger to the widow offering her a choice of either £1000 or a pension of £300 a year for life in payment for them. Mrs. Oliver accepted the second alternative, but later heard that the King had given some of them as presents to his mistresses and illegitimate children. The good lady was much annoyed at this and expressed her disapproval in no uncertain terms. News of this reached the Court and her annuity was stopped for ever.

JOHN HOSKINS

Many lesser miniaturists were by now in the field, for the art was becoming more and more popular amongst those who could afford such work, but it is not within the scope of the present book to discuss them or their productions. After the Olivers the most outstanding name is that of John Hoskins. Apparently there were two artists of this name, for several contemporary and near-contemporary writers refer to John Hoskins and his son, but so far as the evidence of the actual work is concerned there is little or nothing to enable us to identify it as being by two separate artists. Vertue said that the elder Hoskins signed his work with a monogram consisting of an H with an I drawn straight through its bar, whilst the younger artist signed his work simply I.H., with variations. Dr. G. C. Williamson unreservedly accepted this view, and the fact that such a recognized authority should have been convinced inclines one to accept it as well. In short, one may say that there were doubtless two artists of the same name, father and son, but that it is a matter of great difficulty and contention to separate their respective work. Our knowledge of their lives is particularly slight, and can be summed up by saying that there are very few contemporary references to their work, that the elder man was an uncle of the Coopers, and that he died in February 1664 and was buried in St. Paul's, Covent Garden.

For the sake of convenience I shall speak of them as one artist. Hoskins's miniatures are of a very high order, and form a bridge between the colourful work of Hilliard and the Olivers and the strength and magnificent simplicity of Samuel Cooper. In general, and with the exception of a few individual works, his portrayal of character was more intense than anything that had preceded him. His famous portrait of Henrietta Maria (Plate XXXIII) gives us a very good idea of that Queen's haughty but regal demeanour and at the same time exquisitely portrays the youthful beauty that so completely won the heart of Charles Stuart. Her quick temper and the weak obstinacy that drove this woman to spurn the country of her adoption and its religion, are both lurking in those proud eyes and in the set of her mouth. The realism aimed at by the Olivers is almost complete; the decorative background has given way to a completely natural one, and each detail of the subject and her attire is represented with great clarity and fidelity.

Hoskins just fell short of the delicate treatment of Hilliard and the Olivers, but nevertheless his work enjoyed a great vogue during his lifetime, being more popular, according to Sir Kenelm Digby, than that of Van Dyck himself. In many ways this is understandable, for his work has great charm and is without affectation. His greatest weakness seems to have been in his colours, which are often quite harsh, but in spite of this he took the art of the miniature a step farther forward in its path and he left us many works of great quality.

SAMUEL COOPER

Hoskins's nephew, Samuel Cooper, is held by many to be the most accomplished miniaturist that the world has ever known. So far as realism goes, they are undoubtedly right, for no other miniaturist has ever achieved such intense drama and stark realism, and yet still preserved the art's essential qualities. He was the miniaturist of the Commonwealth and no other artist could have portrayed the stern Puritans so well as he did.

Samuel Cooper was born in London in 1609 and received his tuition in miniature painting from his uncle, John Hoskins. As with Hoskins, we have little information about the artist's life, but Pepys makes many interesting references to him in his diary, and from this we learn a few more facts. The entry for 10 July 1668 reads, "To Cooper's, and there find my wife and W. Hewer and Deb., sitting and painting; and here he do work finely, though I fear it will not be so like as I expected; but now I understand his great skill in music, his playing and setting to the French lute most excellently, and he speaks French, and indeed is an excellent man." R. Graham, writing in 1695, says, "He spent several years of his life abroad, was personally acquainted with the greatest men of France, Holland, and his own country, and by his Works more universally known in all the parts of Christendom." He was certainly highly esteemed by his contemporaries and counted such famous men as Milton, Samuel Butler, and Thomas Hobbes among his friends. He worked in many parts of the provinces as well as in London, where his headquarters were in Henrietta Street, Covent Garden. He died on 5 May 1672.

Of Cooper's work, Walpole wrote: "If his portrait of Cromwell could be enlarged to the size of one of Vandyck's pictures, I do not know but Vandyck would appear less great by comparison." High praise indeed! But not undeserved, for to infuse such a strong sense of drama into such small portraits was the work of a master brush. No other artist has been able to do so much before or since. One has only to look at one of his likenesses to have an impression of the sitter's personality marked indelibly in one's mind. Complete realism had been achieved in something like a hundred years from the time of the lyrical Hilliard, and so superbly executed is Cooper's work that it is no exaggeration to suggest that he has said the last word in this direction.

It is useless to try to describe in words the subtlety of this artist's work; it has to be seen to be believed. Look at his masterly portrait of a man, possibly Sir R. Henley (Plate XXXIII), and note the kindly pride in that fine face. There is no artifice, no affectation, no concession to fancy; merely a plain statement of fact—but fact as only a great artist can state it, fact more subtle and more complete than any photograph can portray—a classic simplicity such as is to be found in the work of few men. The same may be said of his portrait of a lady, supposed to be Henrietta, Duchess of Orleans (Plate IV). The same grandeur of conception is here, but at the same time none of the sitter's essential femininity is lost to us. She is still the courtly lady, with a sense of her position and a grace and charm that many a more effeminate painter might have striven in vain to portray.

Samuel Cooper certainly extended the work of the miniature beyond its decorative functions, but he did it with such effortless and masterly skill that there is no sense of strain and he gave the art another facet which it could not have possessed without him. Little wonder that he is acclaimed by many to be the world's greatest limner!

Any miniaturist coming immediately after Cooper would have seemed an anticlimax, but in general the artists that did follow him really were of comparatively poor quality. However there were some good artists practising in the medium at the time, and hosts of lesser ones. Some at their best did good work, but all appear overshadowed by Cooper. Realism had come to stay for the time being, and it was to be a long time before idealism was to be introduced again to any great extent.

THOMAS FLATMAN

The finest miniaturist of the group following Cooper was undoubtedly Thomas Flatman, who, besides being an artist, was also a barrister and poet. According to Horace Walpole, he was born in 1637 in Aldersgate Street, London. He was elected a Scholar and later a Fellow of New College, Oxford. In 1657, he entered the Inner Temple, and after taking his M.A. in Cambridge, by King's letters, was called to the bar. He married in 1672, and settled near Diss, in Norfolk. He died in London on 8th December 1688.

An example of his work, a miniature of Charles II (Plate XXXV), is in the Wallace Collection. One feels, however, that he has not summed up the true character of "Old Rowley," and that he lacks Cooper's perceptive power as a portrait painter. Here is only the sneering side of the monarch's character —certainly not his happy-go-lucky and humorous traits, which were really more typical of him than his cynicism. The miniature is technically impeccable but is nevertheless without much depth.

Of much finer quality is his self-portrait (Plate XXXIV) in the Victoria and Albert Museum. This work is of the highest order in every way and is certainly one of his best productions. The placing of the head within the oval, the rendering of the hair and clothes, and the colouring all combine to make it a successful decorative entity. It is full of character (the artist obviously knew himself) and is completely free from affectation. Another miniature of equal merit, a portrait of a lady, said to be the artist's wife (Plate XXXIV), is in the same collection. The identification of the sitter as his wife seems doubtful, for he did not meet her until 1672, whereas the miniature was executed in 1661.

BERNARD LENS

Another miniaturist of a little later date than Flatman was Bernard Lens, who is reputed to be the first miniaturist to paint on ivory. This artist was born in London in 1682, and was of Dutch descent on his father's side. He received his training at the Academy of Painting in Great Queen Street, Lincoln's Inn Fields, and in time gained a great reputation, becoming miniature-painter to George I and to George II.

Apparently there were three artists of the name of Bernard Lens. The first was an enamel-painter, the second a drawing-master and mezzotint-engraver and father of the third, who was the famous miniaturist.

Bernard Lens, in addition to giving private instruction in miniature painting (Walpole was amongst his pupils) was also drawing-master at Christ's Hospital, and produced an excellent work, *New Complete Drawing Book*, which was, however, published posthumously. After a period of retirement he died at Knightsbridge on 30 December 1740.

His work is certainly not up to the standard of Flatman's, but it has a decorative value and prettiness, notwithstanding. In its class his portrait of Lady Jane Codd (Plate IV), when a child, has a certain quality of childlike charm, but at the same time one feels that rather less sentimentality would have improved it.

A miniature of a ragged boy, painted in 1744 by his son, Peter Paul Lens (Plate XXII), is of great interest, for it takes us for a change away from the world of fashion. The artist has instilled much pathos into the poor twisted little face and draws one's sympathy to a side of life rarely portrayed in miniatures.

NICHOLAS DIXON

Before passing on to the eighteenth-century revival, two more artists must be mentioned. The first is Nicholas Dixon, who succeeded Samuel Cooper as King's Limner in, or about, 1673. He enjoyed great popularity during his lifetime and executed some good works. This artist has been sometimes confused with John Dixon, the mezzotint-engraver. Very little is known of his life, but he was working as early as the sixteen-sixties. He was very much influenced by Sir Peter Lely, whose pupil he was. George Vertue says,

PLATE IV

SAMUEL COOPER
Supposed Portrait of Henrietta,
Duchess of Orleans

Victoria & Albert Museum, P.110–1910.
Crown copyright.

$2\frac{27}{32} \times 2\frac{3}{16}$ *in.*

BERNARD LENS THE YOUNGER
Lady Jane Codd when a Child
Victoria & Albert Museum, D. 97.
Crown copyright.

$3 \times 2\frac{1}{8}$ *in.*

"Dixon was in his greatest capacity of reputation in King Charles II's times King James and beginning of King William. Afterwards he by his worke, seem'd to decline much before he died." The cause of this decline is doubtless explained by a reverse in his fortunes in 1698, caused by a certain bubble lottery, in which Queen Anne herself was said to be concerned. Nicholas Dixon was still living in 1708, but the date of his death remains unknown.

His portrait of General Charles Churchill (Plate XXXVI), painted about 1685, is an interesting miniature. The work is obviously a good likeness but it betrays that weakness which always seems to follow a period of brilliant realism in painting, and which mistakes a slavish representation of what is seen for the artistic conception of realism combined with deep insight, a quality exemplified in Cooper's work and, to a lesser extent, in Flatman's.

LAURENCE CROSS

The last artist of this period to whom I must make some reference is Laurence Cross, who has sometimes been erroneously called Lewis Cross. This artist was born in 1650 and died in 1724. His work falls into much the same category as Dixon's, although it does, to a certain extent, anticipate the new idealistic qualities which were to be seen in the work of the eighteenth-century miniaturists. A comparison of his portrait, supposed to be of one of the Barons Maynard (Plate XXXVI), painted about 1690, with that of General Churchill, by Dixon, will show this. The attitude of the head in the former, slightly turned aside, with the eyes facing the front, and the painting of the face and hair, all exemplify a new approach. The realism is still there, but a new affectation has been added, the full impact of which was not to be felt until the time of Cosway.

An interesting story of Laurence Cross is told by Horace Walpole in his *Anecdotes of Painting*. A supposed portrait of Mary Stuart, Queen of Scotland, was given by the Duke of Hamilton to Cross to be restored. Cross had his own ideas of beauty and gave Mary a round face, in place of her own oval one. At any rate he founded a tradition for her appearance which became almost as strong as that founded by Holbein of Henry VIII's, except of course that in Cross's case it is entirely erroneous.

RICHARD COSWAY

When Bernard Lens died in 1740, a great revival in the art of the portrait miniature was beginning, and amongst the artists who were responsible for it, none have enjoyed such a reputation as Richard Cosway, R.A. In fact for many years, until a revival of interest took place at the end of the nineteenth century, the name Cosway *was* miniature painting. Every eighteenth-century miniature was indiscriminately ascribed to him, and only passing reference was ever made to the great names of earlier times. Amongst less well-informed people at the present time this attitude persists, and it is no uncommon thing for antique dealers and others to offer a miniature for sale as a Cosway when it bears no more resemblance to his work, excepting in period, than it does to a Hilliard. As a matter of fact a genuine Cosway miniature is a rarity, and if the collector is offered for a few pounds a work reputed to be from his brush he should exercise great caution, for it will almost invariably be by someone else.

Richard Cosway was born at Tiverton, in Devon, in 1740 or 1742.[1] His father, who was of Flemish descent, was headmaster of Blundell's School, Tiverton, where Richard was educated. The boy showed ability for painting at an early age, for when he was less than fourteen he gained the first prize ever offered by the Society of Arts. Two years later he won a prize of thirty guineas offered in a competition. Success soon smiled upon him, for he began to exhibit portraits in 1760, ten years later had become an Associate of the recently-formed Royal Academy, and a year after that was made a full Academician. His popularity was finally established when the Prince of Wales, after admiring a portrait of Mrs. Fitzherbert by Cosway, consented to sit for him himself. After this he went from success to success and painted as many as a dozen or even more miniatures in a day.

Cosway's income was enormous, but his tastes were expensive; and this little painter, with a face like a monkey, soon became one of the colourful characters of his day and well earned his nicknames of "Macaroni," "Cosmetic," and "Billy Dimple." In 1781 he married Maria Hadfield, a Catholic girl and a member of the Florentine Academy, who also practised as a

---

[1] Dr. G. C. Williamson gave the date of his birth as 1742 and his probable place of birth as Okeford, near Bampton; he was certainly baptized there in that year.

miniature painter. Together they lived in the lap of luxury, surrounding themselves with princely treasures and furnishings, and dressed in amazing exaggerations of the contemporary fashions. Cosway's flamboyance is accentuated by the signature he sometimes affixed to his miniatures: "Rders. Cosway, R.A., Armiger Primarius Pictor Serenissimi Principis Walliae." Later in his life this picturesque little man suffered from hallucinations and one of his miniatures of that period is signed even more pompously: "Richard Cosway, R.A. et F.S.A., greatest miniature-painter in the world!" After living to see a decline in his popularity, Richard Cosway died on 4 July 1821. His wife went abroad after his death and founded a scholastic establishment for girls near Milan, living to be created a baroness by the Emperor Francis I in 1834. She died on 5 January 1838.

Cosway's work shows the complete realization of the development towards idealism, and is as far removed from the realism of Samuel Cooper as it could be. It is idealistic in a different way than Hilliard's, for the Elizabethan master was concerned more with a lyrical idealism, whereas Cosway's idealism is one of Court beauties and gallants, powder, rouge, and perfume. One feels that most of his sitters have been flattered, and where comparisons are possible with other more realistic painters this is in many cases fully proved. In common with many other eighteenth-century limners, he made his women too beautiful to be true, his men too handsome and noble to be real. Nevertheless, they all have great charm and great decorative value, and although they often betray careless draughtsmanship they are all pleasing to the eye both in form and in colour.

Cosway worked too easily; therein lies his strength and his weakness. His strength because he was able to dash a portrait on to a leaf of ivory in a few strokes, and his weakness because of his careless technique. No man who produced such a vast quantity of work could maintain a consistently high level, but only a man of Cosway's ability could have produced such a large percentage of charming and colourful miniatures with so little effort.

The miniature of Mrs. Fitzherbert (Plate XXXIX) is a beautiful and typical example of Cosway's work. She was exquisitely beautiful, a woman who would be outstanding in any period, and he has lightly painted her with the greatest economy of technique. And yet it is frail work; the artist was treading a narrow path bordered on each side by a chasm. By a miracle he made a success of it, although one false step would have turned it into a travesty. Those who have tried to copy Cosway's style since his time have always overlooked this. His style was so individual that only he could make a success of it; when he died his style died with him. His portrait of Miss Crofton in the same collection is even more lightly sketched in, and yet the very sketchiness of the rest of the miniature serves to enliven and throw up the face. The miniature is surprisingly complete, but it must have been painted in an amazingly short time since his output often amounted to twelve a day!

Amongst his finest miniatures is a portrait of an unknown man (Plate XXXVIII). More finished than the one just mentioned, it is an inspired piece of decorative painting but, like most of his work, it is deficient in its rendering of character. If Cosway could have devoted a little more time to studying character, he might assuredly have been "the greatest miniature-painter in the world," but in that case he would not have been Cosway. Who could imagine this strange monkey-like little dandy, who delighted in external show, as a penetrating portrayer of character? Let us be thankful for him as he was and for what he has left us; for he left a series of miniatures which have given, and will continue to give, pleasure to many generations.

ANDREW AND NATHANIEL PLIMER

Next come Andrew and Nathaniel Plimer, the former a pupil of Cosway. As with so many other miniature painters, little is known of Nathaniel's life, but we have a comparatively complete record of Andrew's. Andrew Plimer was born at Wellington on 29 December 1763, the son of a watchmaker. Both he and his brother were eventually put to this trade, but they disliked it and ran away, joining a band of gipsies. The gipsies, who owned a menagerie, found the artistic talents of the two brothers invaluable for decorating their vehicles. After a time, however, the brothers decided one day, when the encampment was in Buckingham, to leave it and go to London, and this they did, in spite of the many entreaties and promises of the gipsies. Eventually Nathaniel entered the employment of Henry Bone, the enameller, and Andrew became personal servant to Richard Cosway.

Both Cosway and his wife grew to like the boy; and after a period of domestic employment, Andrew was found by Cosway trying to copy one

PLATE V

ANDREW PLIMER
A Lady, possibly Mrs. Hadfield
Victoria & Albert Museum, P.43–1910.
Crown copyright.

ANDREW PLIMER
An Unknown Lady
Victoria & Albert Museum, P.65–1910.
Crown copyright.

of his miniatures. The famous painter was so impressed with the boy's efforts that he at once sent him to a teacher to learn the art of drawing. He made quick progress; and from the time his lessons ended until 1785 he worked in Cosway's own studio. He then left to set up his own studio at 32 Great Maddox Street, Hanover Square. He moved about a great deal after this, and finally settled in Brighton, where he died on 29 January 1837.

In February 1801, he married Joanna Louise Knight, a sister of Mary Ann Knight, the miniature painter. They had a family of five, four daughters and one son, but the boy died in infancy. Plimer's daughters evidently inherited their mother's noted good looks to judge by his miniatures of them. These girls seem to have been the impulse behind his most frequent mannerism, which was a tendency to exaggeration in the size of his sitters' eyes. His daughters had large eyes, and he was evidently so impressed by them that he could conceive of no beauty without such striking features. Mannerisms are very much in evidence in his work, and are his greatest weakness. He had not the lightness of Cosway to offset them, and he went to far greater lengths than his master to cover his subjects with a gloss of sugary sentimentality. He once, for instance, painted a miniature of his daughter, Selina, when a child, and spoiled an otherwise charming work by giving her a pair of angelic wings!

Like Cosway he was far more concerned with decorative qualities than with character, but when he liked, he could surpass Cosway in his portrayal of the latter, although Cosway was always his superior at light, gay, and decorative representations. That Andrew Plimer could at times portray character with success is to be seen in his miniature of an unknown lady (Plate V). Her feminine charms are not lacking by any means, but she obviously had a sharp tongue and a mind of her own. Viewed technically there is a hardness throughout its surface which one would never find in a Cosway; the light easy touch is lacking, and a more laboured method is evident. On the other hand, his portrait of a lady, thought to be Mrs. Hadfield, approaches the lighter touch of his benefactor.

Generally Plimer was more successful in his portraits of women than of men. This was not surprising, for it was a characteristic of most miniaturists of the period, and the decorative values of the feminine attire of the time lent themselves more obviously to their treatment than did those of the men's clothing, gorgeous though this could be. That he could on occasion paint men's portraits as well as he painted women's may be seen by a glance at those reproduced here.

Nathaniel Plimer's miniatures are scarcer than those of his brother, and on the whole are inferior, but he could rise above him in every respect in his better individual works, as in the portrait of Alexander Sprot (this may possibly be Dr. Adam Sprott, Plate XXXVI). In this work, character, a gem-like decorative value and fine execution, all combine to make a near-perfect work. If Nathaniel Plimer had maintained this high standard in all his work he would not only have surpassed his brother but would have come down to posterity as one of the best miniaturists of the eighteenth century.

GEORGE ENGLEHEART

Cosway, as we already know, was miniaturist to the Prince of Wales and his Court. To the more respectable, less fast-moving, Court of the King, the official miniaturist was George Engleheart, a far quieter man than the gay Cosway, as befitted his position, but in every way his equal as an artist. George Engleheart was born at Kew in 1752. He became a pupil of George Banett, R.A., and from that artist learned the technique of water-colour painting. Later he became a pupil of Sir Joshua Reynolds and the two men were destined to become great friends. The President of the Royal Academy had an enormous influence on Engleheart's work, and permitted him to make many copies in miniature of his oil paintings.

According to Engleheart's fee-books, he set up as an independent artist in 1775. This priceless book of records lists some 4853 miniatures by the artist, and shows that, whilst at the beginning of his career he charged but three or four guineas apiece for them, by the end of his working days he commanded prices as high as twenty-five guineas—a large sum for such work in those days. He invested his earnings wisely, and was thus enabled to live in comfort throughout his retirement and to leave a handsome sum to his dependants. He began exhibiting his work at the Royal Academy in 1773 and continued to show there regularly for many years. He married twice, outliving both his wives, and died at Blackheath in 1829.

Technically, his work comes at a point mid-way between Cosway's and Andrew Plimer's. It has not the scintillating brilliance of the former, neither has it the hard and exaggerated qualities of the Plimers. Its finish is much finer than Cosway's and seems to have been more deliberately painted, having a more solid appearance and much more accurate draughtsmanship behind it. Perhaps Reynold's great influence accounts for this. His portrayals of character are far more profound, and his decorative qualities are really much sounder than Cosway's in spite of the latter's brilliance. At a superficial glance, however, much of his work resembles that of Cosway. His portrait of Charlotte-Augusta, Princess Royal (Plate XL), is a case in point, but on closer inspection it will be seen that there are greater depths of modelling, and, although there is still rather an exaggerated prettiness about it, there is more awareness of the underlying character. His more successful work was accomplished in a style more completely his own, of the type illustrated here in the portrait of an unknown lady (Plate XLI), painted about 1780. In this he has given his sitter real character and fully exploited her feminine charms, but at the same time it shows a departure from the idealism of Cosway and the Plimers, and an advance towards realism once again. The idealism of Cosway and others of his time could not last for long. Their idealism was one of artificiality and was bound to change with fashion, and here, in their very midst, was an artist already moving away from it. An even more definite advance in this direction was being made by John Smart, but more will be said of this artist shortly. In the miniature just mentioned, Engleheart displayed his amazing decorative gifts. He rose to the heights of some of the best Elizabethan limners in this respect, and nowhere does he display his powers better than here. It is, however, based on a different approach. Hilliard and his contemporaries founded their decorative approach on pure line and colour, but Engleheart founded his on realistic modelling, skilful posing (one of Andrew Plimer's great weaknesses), and pleasant, but less obvious, harmonies of colour. Once again we see a different approach and two distinct ways of being right.

His portrait of Mr. J. D. Collier (Plate XL), painted about ten years later than that of an unknown lady, shows an even more definite portrayal of character, and at the same time achieves equal decorative success—no affectation, no unreality, but a truthful record of the man's appearance and character. The open face with its half-smiling expression must surely be a true portrait. This work indeed belongs to the highest category.

JOHN SMART

Of the realistic miniaturists of the eighteenth century John Smart was undoubtedly the finest, and although his miniatures have never enjoyed the popularity of Cosway and Engleheart, perhaps because their merits are not so apparent at a first glance, he is unsurpassed in the whole of the eighteenth century either in his portrayals of character or in sheer honest representation. His technique was of a very high order and only surpassed in excellence of finish by John Bogle, whose work will be discussed next. In true nobility, however, the works of John Smart are in a class of their own.

This artist was born in Norfolk, near Norwich, on 1 May 1741.[1] Little is known of his career, but we do know that he came to London and was a pupil of the miniaturist, Daniel Dodd, and that after this he entered St. Martin's Lane Academy. Cosway was certainly among those who gave him instruction, but the results show an approach to miniature painting as different from that of the Academician's as it is from that of Hilliard. This certainly points to the conclusion that the instruction was either very limited or was very little attended to; we should be thankful that this was so, for whereas we might have had just another idealist of the usual eighteenth-century pattern we have one of the greatest realists in the art's history, at a period in which idealism was the order of the day, thus giving double interest to an already intensely interesting epoch. "Honest John Smart," as Cosway called him, was hardly the person to obtain Cosway's brilliant sparkle, for he was an intensely religious man and somehow in his straightforward and somewhat Puritan representations of his sitters we are curiously reminded of Cooper, that other great realist.

In 1785,[2] after a period in which he exhibited frequently at the Royal Academy, Smart went out to India, much to the consternation of Ozias Humphry, who was already there, and who fully realized that the Norfolk man was his superior as an artist. India was a rich working-ground for artists in the eighteenth century, for a fashion of having their portraits painted by European artists had arisen amongst the Indian princes, and Smart did

---

[1] Mr. Arthur Jaffe, a collector who has made a study of Smart's work, believes that this date may be 1742 or 1743.
[2] Dr. Williamson gives this date as 1788.

much of his best work there. It is usually possible to identify which of his miniatures were painted in India, for he almost invariably put the letter "I" beneath his initials on such works. Smart's main working centre in India was Madras, whereas Humphry's was Calcutta.

After a period of great success in India (a success which he had not enjoyed in his own country), John Smart returned to England in 1794, after which he was lucky enough to become friendly with one Toussaint, another miniature painter, and also a jeweller of great ability, who designed and made some really beautiful frames for Smart's miniatures, which served to enhance their already jewel-like appearance. Smart died in London on his birthday in 1811, having become, aesthetically, the finest miniaturist of his generation.

"An Unknown Lady" (Plate XXXVII), painted in 1779, is a fine example of his work, and a really wonderful miniature. In every way a jewel, it has decorative qualities far sounder than, though not so apparent as, those in Cosway's work. The expression on the face is so lively and the whole is painted with such vitality that it brings the presence of the sitter to the eyes of the viewer in an amazingly convincing manner. With the exception of Cooper, no other artist in the whole history of the art has the ability to do this so successfully, nor so often, as Smart, and such a gift lifts the miniaturist above his period and places him on a "timeless" level. Although Smart's sitters are unmistakably of the eighteenth century, his work itself is of more than transitory historical value, and the fact that he worked at that time is beside the point. He would have shone at any period.

Smart's self-portrait (Plate XXXVII) is a masterpiece of characterization. One has only to look at this to see that Cosway's nickname of "Honest John" was a true description of the man, although it may have been meant only as a quip. The kindly face, good-looking but not handsome, shines with honesty. The bare facts that we possess concerning the artist's life are surely compensated for here. It is a portrait so complete that the details are hardly necessary. He was not afraid to show how his coat rumpled—he did not try to gloss it over and make it fit him as if he were a tailor's dummy, as was the practice of so many of his contemporaries—but was content to represent it for posterity exactly as it was. Neither was he afraid to paint in his wrinkles and by so doing betray his age. Without being niggling he has recorded every detail as faithfully as any painter of the age of Ruskin.

His "Girl in White" (Plate XXXVII), in the Wallace Collection, is not up to the standard of the two just mentioned, and is much stiffer and harder in appearance. In this work he just misses the glowing delineation of presence usually associated with him, and seems to have striven for his effects more consciously, with less successful results. Nevertheless, it is a charming little work, and one of which many a lesser artist would have been proud. But it is not Smart at his best. The greatest artists have periods when their work is not at its best, and that he could paint imperfect works is yet another proof of "Honest John's" realism, for he was a human being as well as an artist, with his feet firmly planted on the ground. He obviously painted exactly as he felt, and his reactions to his sitters were not always the same. Cosway painted with a fairly uniform brilliance, but his work is altogether too brilliant. At his best, Smart painted like the great master he undoubtedly was, combining all the requirements of the miniature in nicely balanced proportions. At his second best he was still a miniaturist of the front rank, but with a modicum of artificiality.

JOHN BOGLE

We have already mentioned the brilliant technique of John Bogle, technique that by itself would merit him a place in any history of miniature painting. He is often relegated to a very secondary place in such histories, but although he is not of the greatest stature he is certainly worthy of more attention than he has hitherto been accorded. Perhaps it is because even less is known of him personally than of many other miniaturists.

Of Scottish origin, he exhibited at the Royal Academy from 1772 to 1794, and was working at a later date than this, for miniatures by him dated after 1794 are known. He has been described as being small, lame, very poor and proud, and it is said that he died in great poverty. Beyond this we know practically nothing of his life. Although it is annoying to an antiquarian to know so little of him, his work in itself is sufficient for the connoisseur.

One of his most remarkable works, "The Dutch Governor of Trincomalee" (Plate VI), is in the Salting Collection. For sheer impeccable finish it would be difficult to find an equal to this miniature. In fact it is so finely painted that it is almost impossible to believe that human hands have touched it: it is as clear and uniform as the surface of the finest enamel. This fact by itself is insufficient to justify it as a work of art, for of course excellence of technique should never be an artist's only aim. But in the hands of such a painter as Bogle it assumes an important place in his art; and in this case it is combined with a feeling of immediacy and intimacy to produce an out-standing piece of painting. Its decorative value is obvious too, but somehow it just misses that final strength that puts such a vivid hallmark upon Smart's work. With Smart's master touch and insight into character, Bogle might have been that artist's equal. He was without these final qualifications, and his work has come down to us as of the finest workmanship, but without the most penetrating insight.

OZIAS HUMPHRY

The last painter of this important period whose work I shall discuss is Ozias Humphry, R.A.; certainly not a miniaturist of the very highest level, but at least one who could rise to high things when the spirit moved him. His birthplace was Honiton, where his mother had a successful business as a lace-maker. On discovering that the boy had artistic leanings and a certain ability in that direction, his father sent him to study at Shipley's School in St. Martin's Lane, London. He returned to Devon, however, on his father's death, and after a short while went to Bath in 1762, where he served an apprenticeship to the miniaturist, Samuel Collins. Later, he returned to London and obtained an interview with Sir Joshua Reynolds, who gave him encouragement and persuaded him to start his own practice. The idea appealed to Humphry, and after another visit to Bath (upon which began a friendship with Gainsborough), he settled in London, with rooms in Covent Garden.

He obtained commissions to paint members of the Royal Family at an early date (1766), and seems to have met with some success. But he felt an urge to travel and make his fortune abroad; and after travelling for a while in Europe (accompanied part of the time by Romney) he decided to go to India and try his fortune there. He went in 1785, and was not long in ob-taining a vast amount of work. The great fortune he had expected to make was, however, not forthcoming, for the princes were much fonder of giving orders than of paying for them. The result of this was that the miniaturist returned to this country in 1788, broken in health and spirit. He was elected an R.A. in 1791, and a year later became an official portrait-painter to

George III. The latter position only covered his work as a painter in crayons and was not really an official recognition of his work as a miniaturist. He died in 1810.

Humphry's best work was that which he left in what he would have considered an unfinished state. With the subsequent "finish" which he imparted to his other work he only succeeded in hiding the original vitality of the first inspiration. In this he anticipated the Victorian miniaturists, most of whom were destined to overpaint to an alarming degree. It is heart-rending to think of how much good work he might have left us, if he had only been aware of this.

He was an exponent of realism rather than of idealism, although the latter is present to a greater or lesser degree in most of his work. Only occasionally does he capture that elusive presence and drawing of character which are the greatest attributes of his contemporary and rival, John Smart; and he but rarely approaches the sparkle of Cosway's light-hearted miniatures. Moreover he was a mannerist in much the same way as Andrew Plimer, but with different results. Plimer exaggerated the largeness of his sitter's eyes, Humphry their smallness. This characteristic gives many of his subjects a mean appearance, and is anything but flattering to them. Nevertheless, in spite of all these defects, this artist's work has a charm of its own and is well worth the attention of both the student and the collector. He was a better painter than almost any of the nineteenth-century school, and in fact, if he had lived but a generation later, he would have been an outstanding miniaturist. As it was he was born and he worked in one of the art's greatest periods and inevitably suffers by comparison with such a giant as Smart or with a painter of such obvious charms as Cosway (Plate VI).

THE NINETEENTH-CENTURY DECLINE

The next period is one which is noted for an aesthetic weakening in all branches of the fine arts, with a corresponding increase in technical impeccability. The prospects of British art looked bright at the beginning of the nineteenth century. Blake, Constable, Turner, Gainsborough, Reynolds, and many others were either at work or had only recently stopped working in the larger types of painting, and art showed more promise in these islands than at any time since the Middle Ages. In miniature painting the artists

PLATE VI

JOHN BOGLE

The Dutch Governor of Trincomalee

Victoria & Albert Museum, P.83–1910.
Crown copyright.

OZIAS HUMPHRY, R.A.

George Harry, Fifth Earl of Stamford

Victoria & Albert Museum, P.23–1937.
Crown copyright.

4 × 3¼ in.

SIR W. C. ROSS, R.A.

The Painter Himself

Victoria & Albert Museum, 1384–1874.
Crown copyright.

whom we have just been discussing exercised a powerful influence and appeared to have founded a school which would have a lasting effect for many generations at least. By the second half of the nineteenth century, however, their influence had almost faded away and the art of the miniature was all but dead. Constable and Turner had given place to Frith and Goodall; Gainsborough and Reynolds to Baxter and Leighton; Blake to G. F. Watts; whilst Smart, Cosway, and Engleheart, and all the host of outstanding eighteenth-century miniaturists, had been replaced by such painters as Sir William Charles Ross and J. C. D. Engleheart.

Doubtless, so far as the miniature is concerned, this decline was hastened by the invention and subsequent popularity of the daguerreotype. Photographs gave a likeness for much less cost than the average miniature. It did not matter that it was uncoloured and that it could only give a transient glimpse of one aspect of the sitter's character—it was accepted and became popular. This was just one symptom of the general decline in taste that was ushered in with the doubtful benefits of mass-production and the new industrial age. We are indeed lucky that the art has managed to survive at all until our own time, but the story of its survival must be reserved for the next chapter.

SIR WILLIAM ROSS

Sir William Charles Ross, R.A., was a typical artist of the time. He was born in London in 1794, his father, once a miniaturist, being a gardener to the Duke of Marlborough. His mother, too, had an artistic streak in her, for she was a daughter of the engraver, Anker Smith, and is known to have painted portraits herself. Young Ross must have had some ability at an early age, for the Royal Academy accepted three genre paintings by him when he was only fifteen years old. For some time his ambition lay in this direction, but miniature painting attracted him, and in 1814 he became a pupil of Andrew Robertson, a miniaturist of some merit, but one who tried to strain the medium beyond its limits by trying to make water-colour resemble oil. Ross was elected an A.R.A. in 1838, and an Academician during the following year. He reached a high degree of popularity as a fashionable portrait-painter, and must be reckoned as the last really popular artist in the medium of miniature painting. He died in London on 20 January 1860.

An interesting early miniature by Ross is in the Victoria and Albert Museum. This is a self-portrait (Plate VI), executed in 1815. In its essentials it is little different from the type produced by the lesser men of the preceding period, although it has a stiffer method of execution—a trait that was to make his work so lifeless in the years to come. The stiffness in the portrait could perhaps be attributed to the fact that it was the work of an artist still in his formative period, but even if this were so, there is no doubt that Ross took the wrong turning at a later date and, like most Victorian painters, over-finished his work, giving it an unhealthy waxwork-like appearance.

His portrait of Harriet, Countess Gower, afterwards Duchess of Sutherland (Plate XLIV), illustrates this defect completely. Overpainted, overposed, and overdressed, this miniature gives a more eloquent summing up of Victorian miniature painting than any words could do. It has not so much the appearance of a painting as that of a carefully posed photograph, with just the right positioning of the head (carefully chosen to show the "beautiful lady") and just the right amount of faultless bosom; yes—even the noble pillar! "Is this," one may well ask, "the work of a countryman of John Smart, working but a few decades after his time?" It was clear that the art had sunk to depths which would have been considered impossible seventy years before.

Ross made wide use of the new method of painting on larger pieces of ivory than had been found possible hitherto. To prepare these large pieces of ivory, shavings were cut from the circumference of a tusk and pressed out flat. The drawback was that they were always straining to resume their natural shape, with the result that they cracked or cockled. In using such large pieces of ivory Ross was taking miniature painting beyond its limits, quite apart from the technical drawback just mentioned, and this alone was symptomatic of the art's decline.

J. C. D. ENGLEHEART

An artist of far greater charm than Ross was his contemporary, John Cox Dillman Engleheart. In many ways this artist's work might have been the product of the eighteenth century, rather than the nineteenth. It combined the idealized vision of the former with the hard colouring of the latter. J. C. D. Engleheart was born in 1784 and was a nephew of the greater George

Engleheart, whose pupil he was. After working for some time under his uncle's instructions he set up to practise on his own, with his headquarters near Oxford Street, later moving to various other places in London. He enjoyed a considerable success and reputation during his lifetime, although his work declined in quality as the years went by. He died at Tunbridge Wells in 1862.

The example of his work reproduced here, a portrait of a girl, said to be Miss Mary Engleheart (Plate XLII), is one of his better works. But it does not require much perception to see a hardening of the general outlook and the intrusion of a mechanical vision, as opposed to imaginative realism. The granulated effect of the background is in many ways typical of certain trends amongst nineteenth-century miniature painters, and betrays a coarsening of the art's technique.

This coarsening was seized upon by some artists, and turned with success into a suitable variation in the medium of miniature painting. But for the coming of photography the miniature would probably have developed along these lines and produced an entirely new school of limners. It will be seen in the next chapter that some contemporary miniaturists are working with success along such paths, but whether this will prove to be the miniaturist's regular technique in the future is questionable, for an entirely new beginning has had to be made and we are almost creating our own standards. It is most unlikely, however, that this would have happened if the best nineteenth-century miniaturists had been followed up by a numerous school.

JOHN LINNELL

John Linnell was a miniaturist who used this new development in technique, and without doubt his work is some of the best to have been produced in nineteenth-century England. He was born in Bloomsbury in 1792, the son of a picture-dealer. A pupil of Blake, Varley, and Godwin, he was a great lover of landscape painting, and regarded portraiture merely as his bread and butter. In fact he gave up portrait painting altogether at the age of fifty-five, and spent the greater part of his remaining years painting landscapes in Surrey. Although he first exhibited at the Royal Academy at the age of fifteen and continued to do so for seventy-four years, he was never elected to that body. He died at Redhill in 1882.

"An Unknown Man" (Plate XLII), painted about 1825 and reproduced here, is a fine example of his work. It has a finely-drawn character and is beautifully painted. Certainly, it achieves much more than the work of Ross, in spite of the latter's high polish. It is exasperating to a lover of miniatures to think what work might have been done in a school of limning with this type of work as a foundation, in a more enlightened age. But let us not be too hard on the Victorians; they are not really to be blamed for thinking more of their fascinating new inventions than of their art. Who could have foreseen what their relative values were to be in the years to come? We can only thank Providence that the work of artists like Linnell was not stifled altogether in the prevailing lack of good taste.

SIMON JACQUES ROCHARD

Lastly we come to Simon Jacques Rochard, a French artist, who was born in Paris in 1788, and, after being a pupil of Isabey, the French miniaturist, began practising the art in England in 1815, and did the best of his work here. He died in Brussels in 1872.

Rochard was also an exponent of the broader technique. Like Ross, he inclined to the use of large ivories, and showed the same technical short-comings; but his work, unlike that of Ross, has great charm. His portrait of Miss and Master Stirling (Plate XLIII), painted in 1826, is one of the best miniatures of the nineteenth century. The grouping of the two children and the whole composition of the piece is cleverly accomplished, and it attains an intimacy sadly missing from so many of its contemporaries. It is definitely an idealized miniature, but not of the simpering, sentimental type; it is lyrical, not as the Elizabethan work was lyrical but in the sense that it is a pretty little picture of brother and sister, obviously on affectionate terms with each other, and conveys successfully the idea of a charming relationship.

On this pleasing note of charm and intimacy, let us leave this period, which was the last until the art's revival at the end of the century.

CHAPTER FOUR

Revival and the Contemporary School

THE tremendous setback which the art received in the nineteenth century seemed to leave it without any hope for the future. The inferior work produced by such painters as Ross and J. C. D. Engleheart was no match for the newly-invented photograph, which could give a likeness for a fraction of the cost of a miniature. With greater artists handling its destinies the miniature might have successfully combated its formidable new rival; but that was not to be and only a small trickle of artists managed to keep it alive at all. It became the toy of the dilettante and ceased to be a living art. Moreover, like so many other arts and crafts in the nineteenth century, it was listed amongst the polite accomplishments of young ladies of leisure, with results that are best left to the imagination. An art which had witnessed the high achievements of Hilliard, Cooper, and Smart degenerated into a milk-and-water sentimentality in comparison with which the sentimental mannerisms of Andrew Plimer and Richard Cosway look like profound psychological studies.

Fortunately, however, there were still some who had the true interests of the art in mind, and a revival of interest in its history began to take place when books like Dr. Lumsden Propert's *History of Miniature Art* appeared in the 'eighties. A study of an art's history is the surest way to provide a firm foundation for future work, and until such scholars as Dr. Propert began to reconstruct it the history of miniature painting had been completely forgotten by the Victorian age. Cosway's was the only name ever heard, and that was doubtless due to his eccentric characteristics as a person, rather than to his art. In such circumstances good work was not likely to be forthcoming from even the most skilled artists. It is significant that soon after Dr. Propert's work was published the revival began to take place. Momentum was added to the awakening interest by the books of Dr. G. C. Williamson and J. J. Foster, which began to appear from ten to fifteen years later, when serious-minded artists were again practising miniature painting with some success.

THE TWO SOCIETIES

The turning-point came in 1895, when two societies were formed for the especial benefit of miniature painters: the Society of Miniature Painters and the Society of Miniaturists. The former was founded by the late Alyn Williams, and the latter by the late Alfred Praga, who was its President until his death in 1949. Both societies are operating to-day. It was a pity that they began by quarrelling bitterly as to which of the two was formed first and which was consequently entitled to style itself the Society of Miniature Painters. At a time when the future of the art was in the balance, co-operation should have been the order of the day, for one combined society could have achieved far more than two divided groups. But quarrel they did, and it was some years before bygones were allowed to be bygones. Now a much more friendly atmosphere prevails, and it is to be hoped that this state of things will continue.

The Society of Miniature Painters grew in strength and popularity, until in 1905 it was granted the title "Royal" by King Edward VII. Later still, its title was augmented, by command of King George V, to the Royal Society of Miniature Painters, Sculptors and Gravers, thus widening its scope to include other artists in little, in addition to painters. The other society grew likewise, although it has still retained its original title, and to-day they both hold annual exhibitions in London.

THE CONTEMPORARY SCHOOL

It would be idle to pretend that we have a school of miniature painting to-day which will stand comparison with what was being done in the past, up to the end of the eighteenth century; but we have individual painters who are infinitely better than most of the Victorian miniaturists, and who are the equals of many of the lesser artists of times preceding that. Generally speaking, technique is of a high order and taste is sound. At the same time interest in the art is still slowly on the increase. If full use is made of available talent and some of the recent developments in larger painting are assimilated—not forgetting the miniature's own traditions, however—great things may again be achieved. Since the revival, solid progress has been made and we now have a large number of practising miniaturists who have a high degree of competence, and quite a few others who have considerably more than competence. Moreover, a fair proportion derive their income solely from miniature painting; this is indeed a good sign, for it shows that there is still a social demand and justification for it. But there is not a school in the strict meaning of the word—there is too great a variety of styles for that. Miniaturists have still to find a common denominator in contemporary painting. It is natural that this should be so, because we are still gathering up the threads of tradition and have hardly had time to look at the future, but the time is fast approaching when we must face the fact squarely, and tune our art in complete accordance with modern tastes and requirements.

So far as the portrait miniature is concerned, the contemporary group is fairly evenly divided into two parts, realistic and idealistic painters. Of the former Lisa de Montfort is an outstanding example, and of the latter Joan Ayling. Working in a class between the two is Marjory Forbes. The realistic group is numerically the smaller, but the idealistic group is often tainted by an over-sentimental attitude, which brings the number of its artistically successful working members down to about the same size as the realistic group. Which of the two will be regarded by posterity as the better, it is difficult to say. For one thing fashions change so much, and where one period will accept Hilliard's work as the greatest achievement of miniature portraiture, in another he and his contemporaries will be superseded in popularity by the great names of, for example, the eighteenth century. Doubtless the best attitude to maintain is one of catholicity, which will enable the student to maintain a sympathetic view of the work of the painters of all periods and styles and to judge the work of the individual miniaturist by the standards of his own class.

LISA DE MONTFORT

Lisa de Montfort first came to England in 1921, after spending her earliest years in South Africa, where she was born. She first painted miniatures in 1939, with most successful results, for to a greater extent than any other contemporary miniaturist she possesses the gift of suggesting the presence of her sitters. Her interpretations of their characters are also of a high quality. Technically her work is interesting, for she works in oils and not in watercolours, as is the usual practice in miniature painting. Oil-colours have certainly been used in the past at most stages of the art's development, but their use has been far more restricted than that of water-colours. They are not generally so suitable, on account of their sticky quality, but Lisa de Montfort has fully overcome this drawback, and her work misses none of the minute handling of miniatures executed in the more usual medium.

Her portrait of John Pemberton (Plate XLV) is one of her best works, and fully illustrates all her good qualities. The minute painting of every detail, without any fussiness, however, and the fine modelling of the face together make this work a masterly piece of portraiture. But the truly remarkable feature of the miniature is the way in which the presence of the sitter is so forcibly brought to the viewer. Even in a monochrome reproduction he is just as truly present as if a mirror were being held up to his features. The work also has obvious decorative qualities.

In her portrait of Meum Stewart (Plate XLV) she explores her decorative abilities even further, and introduces a pleasant little landscape as a background to her sitter, whose presence is conveyed no less unmistakably than in the last work. Miss de Montfort has fully exploited the uses of backgrounds in miniatures, and often uses them to portray the occupations, or other interests, of her sitters, as in the miniature of Etienne Amyot (Plate XLVII), where a grand piano is significantly, but not obtrusively, placed in the distance.

Lisa de Montfort stands at the present time in a class of her own, a realist miniature painter of the first rank, combining realistic vision with imaginative qualities. It would be difficult to overestimate the importance of her work at a time when the art is at the most critical period in its history. Her miniatures stand as a pointer to the path which realist portrait miniaturists must tread, if they are to make that side of the art of first-class importance once again.

MARJORY FORBES

In Marjory Forbes we have an artist who, whilst essentially still a realist, partakes more fully of the idealistic attitude towards her subjects than does Lisa de Montfort. Her miniatures are still straightforward pieces of portraiture, but they have a lyrical quality which, however small it may be, takes a step away from the truly realist group. If Miss de Montfort finds her antecedents in Cooper and his contemporaries, then Miss Forbes finds hers in George Engleheart and his circle.[1] In addition she lays far more emphasis on the decorative function of her work than Lisa de Montfort does in hers. Her technique consists mainly in the use of light washes, which in spite of their lightness are far from insipid, bringing into her work a sparkle and limpidity rarely seen since the close of the eighteenth century.

The miniature of Sheila Ann Mackinnon (Plate XLVI) is a particularly delightful example of Marjory Forbes's ability to combine realism with decoration and at the same time to infuse an imaginative lyricism into the whole. A glance will show that this is realism of a different cast from that of Lisa de Montfort. The arrangement and painting of the hair, for example, show that this artist has her eyes wide open to the purely decorative aspect of her work, whilst the whole is definitely a partially idealized conception. Do not misunderstand this statement. It is far, far removed from the simpering mock-angels so often passed off as children, and is idealized in the best sense of the word—in the sense that this little girl's portrait is an ideal conception of her appearance; not a simple statement, but a translation. In selecting a middle path, the artist is just as much within the bounds of law as if she were either a definite realist or a definite idealist.

In a more realistic key is "Bridget" (Plate XLVI), although decorative values have been fully exploited here too, both in its colouring and in its conception. It shows the artist in an entirely different mood from that of the portrait of Sheila Ann Mackinnon, and also shows that no set rule can be applied absolutely to any painter. It indicates in addition that Marjory Forbes does not allow herself to get into a rut and is as capable in a miniature of this class as she is in one that leans further towards idealism.

JOAN AYLING

Joan Ayling's works are the most lyrical and truly idealistic portrait miniatures being painted to-day. Almost alone amongst modern idealist portrait miniaturists, she has succeeded in bringing true imagination into her work, without getting lost in a mire of pretty and gushing flattery. Lisa de Montfort, as

---

[1] It is, perhaps, only fair to state here that Miss Forbes herself claims Holbein and Hilliard as her chief historical influence. I must say, however, that her work strikes me as showing far more the influence of eighteenth-century sources.

I have already said, shows the true path for the painter of realist portrait miniatures, and equally Joan Ayling points the way for those in the other group. Both types can flourish side by side in perfect equanimity, but it must be realized that the attitude of each is as different as can be from the other. Joan Ayling's work is founded upon the same tenets as those of the Elizabethan school. These call for a translation of the sitter's appearance and character into terms of paint, founded on a basis of line and pure colour. On the other hand, the realist's aim is to give an accurate visual record of the sitter's appearance and character.

Miss Ayling shows a bold approach to her particular problems and possesses a strength of line and purity of colour all too rarely seen to-day. In her translations of forms into the simplest shapes compatible with her medium, she shows that she has a truly modern vision, yet at the same time she never loses sight of the art's traditions. "Ann" (Plate XLIX) is an example. The hair is simplified into a series of locks, and the face, though perfectly modelled, goes through much the same process. Character is there, and presence, but these are not her first considerations. The whole miniature is a clear statement of the subject's appearance in decorative terms, and it would figure equally well either as a picture in its own right or as an embellishment to a more general decorative scheme, for example, in an illuminated manuscript or in a piece of jewellery.

In similar mood is the same artist's "Eleonore in Fancy Dress" (Plate XLVIII). This miniature shows that Joan Ayling is not afraid of more complicated compositions, which she uses without striving for the grandiose. Yet in it she does paint a much more convincing aspect of Victoriana than any Victorian miniaturist ever did, and with much more sympathy for the period. The Victorians left us a legacy of pomp and circumstance, bourgeois respectability, and jingoism; but they also had an unmistakably fantastic side, and here Joan Ayling puts it on record in a charming manner, but completely through the vision of a twentieth-century observer. The curtain and the prancing horse in the background add a pleasant theatrical note to this most satisfying little work.

"Rai" (Plate XLIX) is one of Miss Ayling's earlier works, and shows her at a time before she had fully assimilated her debt to the Elizabethans and asserted the complete originality she shows at the present time. None the less, it is a pretty little work, and I include it both because of this, and because it shows unmistakably that the artist based her approach from the first upon the idealist vision of Hilliard and the sixteenth-century school.

OTHER MINIATURISTS

Apart from the artists just mentioned, whose work I have particularly discussed because they show in crystallized form the best general trends at the present time, there are many others doing solid and valuable work in the contemporary school. Among realists, Bertram Cocks shows what can be achieved in part-time work. "Sunday painters," as such artists are called, have a great duty to perform in keeping the art of miniature painting alive. Few miniaturists at present can derive their income from this source alone, and it is good to see that an artist like Mr. Cocks is doing such sound and straightforward work in his spare time, thus showing the way to others. In fact many miniaturists who devote their whole time to the art might benefit by paying more attention to straightforward painting and less to sentimentalizing their sitters out of recognition. Edith Davey also aims at a good likeness as her first consideration, and produces good unpretentious portraits. Alice Cook, primarily an enamel-painter, brings a fine technique into her work when she does ordinary miniature painting. She is capable of conveying a convincing sense of presence.

Amongst others are Iris Moncrieff-Bell, whose portrayals of character are very good indeed, and who works in a light effortless manner (Plate L); Kathleen Goodman, who stresses the decorative aspects of the realist miniature (Plate L); Harold Lisle, at his best a fine portrayer of character; Joyce Kilburn, Christiana B. K. May, E. Burnett Crawshaw, Marjorie Rodgers, Nellie Hepburn-Edmunds, and S. Arthur Lindsay. All of these artists and many others of their contemporaries are doing yeoman work, both in keeping the art alive and in laying firm foundations for its future.

I have already said that there are many contemporary miniaturists in the idealist group who over-sentimentalize their sitters, but in addition to Joan Ayling and Marjory Forbes there are quite a number of others who use their imagination in the right way. Notable amongst such is Isabel Saul, who uses realism as a springboard for her decorative idealism. Her portrait, "Mrs. Saul" (Plate LIV), is an excellent miniature of this type. It shows that the artist is not so far along this path as Joan Ayling has travelled, but falls rather more into Marjory Forbes's class. The character and presence of the sitter are forcibly portrayed and bring this work well within the realist class, but the decorative aspect is so fully exploited in the patterning of the dress, the calligraphy, and the actual technique, that it just comes within the second group.

Kathleen Maude, after a varied career, first as a dancer and then as a sculptor, came to miniature painting as late as 1938. In her recent mono-chrome imaginative portraits she has shown how, with wit and a sense of period, these can, at the same time, be effective decoratively. "The Snore" (Plate LI) is a good example of her work. As an illustrative artist she exploits the miniature portrait for the purpose for which the subject miniature first came into being, and shows, with distinct success, that it can be just as serviceable.

The miniatures of Hope Douglas show the influence of the revival of the art in France, which also took place towards the end of the nineteenth century. "Hope Helen" (Plate XLVII) shows her at her best, in an idealized portrait of a little girl. The work of E. Mary Burgess should also be mentioned, for, at its best, it has much the same qualities. Finally I must note the miniatures of Daysi M. Brookes, who is not only doing valuable work in popularizing the art in Australia, but also is producing some pleasing and original work in both groups—particularly the second (Plate LIV).

THE SUBJECT MINIATURE

And what of the subject miniature? How is that faring at the present time? The answer is, quite as well as its admittedly more popular sister-art, but with the same proviso—that much of it is over-sentimentalized to a sickening degree. Like the portrait miniature it is fairly evenly divided into two groups, idealists and realists, both of which put it to its traditional uses, from embellishments in illuminated manuscripts to miniatures in their own right.

ILLUMINATED MINIATURES

There are few illuminators producing good miniatures themselves to-day. Often their work, from a calligraphic standpoint, is good, but as such does not concern us here. Many illuminators solicit the co-operation of other artists to paint their miniatures, as Graily Hewitt has done with Miss Ayling. Such partnerships can be carried out without the result's being a pastiche, but extremely close co-operation is needed to ensure success. Some merely produce writing with gilded and coloured initials, with perhaps a few other sundry pieces of decoration, which are not miniatures. The remainder, with a few exceptions, do decorate their manuscripts with miniatures of varying degrees of quality, and those who rise above the general standard are often capable of really fine work of great feeling, and are in fact responsible for some of the best contemporary idealist subject miniatures.

Amongst the finest contemporary illuminators who paint their own miniatures, my own teacher, Albert Cousins, is outstanding (Plate LVI). His miniatures provide a perfect counterpoint to his calligraphy, and each complements the other to a rare degree. There are those who contend that illumination is a dead art, but to such I would say: "Study the work of Albert Cousins; with such an illuminator in our midst the art could not possibly be dead." He is particularly happy in introducing flower studies into his work, and this he does with great taste and imagination (if only some of the painters of framed flower miniatures had as much!). He is most successful with English spring flowers and is happiest in painting his own favourite crocuses.

Although such an art is purely decorative, Mr. Cousins has not failed to instil a great deal of feeling into his work. Moreover, he has taken his subject-matter from his own experience and has not relied upon making copies of *motifs* taken from earlier work. Building upon traditional sources, he has worked out his own conceptions, with the result that he has brought a breath of fresh air to an art that looked as if its revival was to be all too short-lived.

The illuminated manuscript is still of great value for ceremonial purposes, and to those who appreciate a beautiful thing for its own sake; to such it would indeed be a tragedy if it were to die out. Mr. Cousins has done as much as any living artist—much more than most—to ensure that this does not happen. His humility towards his work, his deep knowledge of its traditions, and his insistence upon the art's foundation on sound craftsmanship, place him amongst the few serious thinkers in the world of miniature painting to-day. His great practical ability has been fully recognized, for many public bodies have commissioned work from him, and examples are to be seen in such places as St. Paul's Cathedral and the Library of Gonville and Caius College, Cambridge, to mention only two of many.

Of those miniaturists who have successfully adapted the illuminated miniature to the frame, Isabel Saul must be specially mentioned. Her work has really first-class decorative and intimate qualities (Plate LVII). Also it is technically original, usually being in the form of coloured and gilded etchings of historical subjects. It is essentially still in the realm of illuminating, and partakes of the calligraphic attitude of its antecedents. Her delicate and nervous line is noteworthy, and her distribution of gold and colour over its surface gives her work decorative entity.

Joyce Kilburn's subject miniatures take us a step farther away from the illuminated miniature, whilst still retaining its idealistic qualities. Her skilful use of the cat's silhouette in "On the Stairs" (Plate LX) shows that Japanese art is amongst her influences. The outline of the cat, the arrangement of its markings, and their relationship to the horizontal lines of the stairs, form an interesting study in composition. Moreover she had shown great originality and success in cutting down the use of perspective to a minimum. This is a feature common to almost all Chinese and Japanese paintings, and with its obvious advantages in dealing with planes instead of solids has been seized upon by many Post-Impressionist painters—sometimes with good and sometimes with bad results. It is of far greater value in limning than in large painting, however, for the flat silhouette can give a much better idea of recession and depth in such small works than elaborate "three-dimensional" painting, which involves the use of shading and a consequent darkening of the colours. Mrs. Kilburn's contribution to the subject miniature has certainly been significant in accentuating this.

An artist who is at roughly the same artistic distance from the illuminator as Joyce Kilburn is Marjorie Rodgers. Her "Masquerade" miniatures (Plate LIX) show the influence of Léon Bakst, whose wonderful designs for the Diaghilev Ballet so dazzled the Western world at the beginning of this century that their influence has been widely diffused ever since. Bakst himself had, in many ways, the spirit of the miniaturist, for his original designs for such ballets as *Le Dieu Bleu*, *Cléopâtre*, and *Sleeping Princess* scintillate with the gem-like brilliance which all good miniatures should possess. It has always been a mystery to me why Bakst has not had a greater influence on modern miniature painting; such an influence would have been of immeasurably greater value than that of the prim Victorians. However, it is good to see that at least one contemporary miniaturist has profited by his example, even though she may have done so unconsciously. Like Joyce Kilburn, Marjorie Rodgers realizes the value of the silhouette and the plain, unshaded space; in addition she has brought into these works a feeling of rhythm and movement, together with an atmosphere that is but a little removed from pure hedonism.

In her floral miniatures she is also well above the average, but in this case her approach is completely realistic, in contrast to the idealist work that we have just been discussing.

THE FLORAL MINIATURE

The sphere of the miniature painters of flowers is, so far as quality goes, a very mixed one, and although there are many who paint excellent miniatures of this kind, there are a far greater number who produce work much inferior to a second-rate print and who confound a pretty surface with a sound work of art. Flowers have personality and character, as the Chinese painters well know, and should be painted with that in view. The miniaturist, even the most ardent realist, has a far greater problem than merely to transfer a super-ficially pretty appearance to the surface of his ivory. Alone amongst subject miniaturists, the flower-painter has almost the same problems as the portrait miniaturist.

Three of our best flower miniaturists, painters who are at the same time typical of vastly different trends in the art, are Mabel Rahbula, Lucy E. Pierce, and Alice Bingham.

Of all contemporary flower miniaturists Mabel Rahbula possesses the most highly polished technique. Her work is an adaptation of the flower paintings of the Dutch masters to the medium of the miniature. She concentrates on the decorative value of her subjects, rather than upon their individuality, but she remains a complete realist. Some may object to her high polish on the grounds that the extremely ephemeral nature of flowers makes them unsuitable to be thus portrayed, but there is room for both light and highly-finished approaches and the highly finished flower miniatures of Mabel Rahbula and Marjorie Rodgers (Plate LV) achieve results which could not be reached by other methods. The laborious method which Mrs. Rahbula uses (for one miniature must take her months to paint) is well disguised by her glittering and jewelled colouring.

Lucy Pierce, who died recently, took a much lighter path as regards technique; this was derived in part from the methods of the illuminator and in part from straightforward water-colour painting. Despite the obvious frailties of such a method, which might well have proved a pitfall to a lesser artist, Miss Pierce derived a most brilliant effect from it, and her colouring had a surprising depth and intensity. Without doubt, she was one of our best floral miniaturists. Her approach to her subjects was truly poetic, and in direct contrast to the realism of Mrs. Rahbula. Much the same may be said of her other work, particularly of her little costume pieces, which are amongst the most charming things of their kind in contemporary miniature painting.

Alice Bingham shows yet another attitude towards the floral miniature, for she uses a method of *premier-coup* painting to serve her purposes. Lighter even than Lucy Pierce in her portrayals, she reproduces in full, and with unmistakable realism, the frail but colourful characters of flowers (Plate LV).

LANDSCAPE MINIATURES

Of landscape painters in miniature, Lieutenant-Colonel F. A. Goddard is the complete realist (Plate LIII). His work closely approaches the picture in little, as distinct from the miniature proper, but falls into the latter class because of its extremely minute finish and jewel-like execution. He paints every detail in his tiny oil paintings with a pre-Raphaelite intensity, and makes every detail play its part in the general design—intense realism is the springboard of his art. An artist working on similar lines, but who uses water-colour instead of oils, is G. London Wood, who was originally a landscape gardener, but who took up miniature painting in his retirement in order to supplement his income. The results have been good, considering that he has been working for only a few years (Plate LII). On the lyrical side, Kathleen Henderson's little Scottish landscapes are of first-rate quality and give pleasant interpretations of the wild and romantic prospects of Iona, where she lives.

Kathleen Maude's subject miniatures are adaptations of the book-illustration to the frame, and are well conceived and executed. They are all of an imaginative character, and would make excellent illustrations for children's books. She seems to have that understanding of the character of animals so common in children, but alas, so rare in adults, and one feels that the spectacle of a rabbit walking on its hindlegs, in one of her miniatures, is no more incongruous than it is in "Alice in Wonderland." An artist with a sense of humour is certainly invaluable in modern miniature painting, when sickly sentiment is so common.

"White Horses" (Plate LVIII), by Rosemary Sutcliff, is a work by another idealist painter. It is one of her best works to date.

THE PRESENT OUTLOOK

What of the future? Will the miniature gain popularity once more or will it die out and be forgotten? The answer to this depends on the artists themselves, their patrons, and their critics. The artist is obviously the most important person of the three, and the longevity of the art ultimately depends upon what he has to offer. As will have been seen from the foregoing, there are miniaturists at work at this moment who are capable of good work, but there must still be more, many more, than these to ensure a promising future. There are still far too many "anecdotal" painters; far too many miniatures of pseudo-romantic subjects, blue-eyed angel children and pretty violets—to say nothing of the arch titles in the catalogues. These bring nothing but disrepute upon an art that has infinitely better things to show at its best.

The miniaturist should not be afraid to experiment. He must either progress or regress, for it is just as impossible to remain at a standstill in this art as it is in any other. Let him look to the future and ask himself frankly if his work is likely to live. Is it just a repetition of what has gone before, or does it show a new approach or a genuine development? If it is a repetition of something that was being done fifty or a hundred or more years ago, it is condemned, at best, to be regarded by posterity as a good piece of craftsmanship, executed without feeling or insight. If it is original, not *novel*, then it stands an excellent chance of survival. Let the contemporary miniaturist benefit by the experiments of the School of Paris and other such modern movements. Let him assimilate them and combine them with his own traditions, to make a school as original as any in the past and not just a thinly scattered movement with comparatively few artists of value here and there. Matisse, Vuillard, Bonnard, Gauguin, Braque, and many others like them who emphasize the decorative value of paints all have valuable lessons to teach us. Let us build up our future by combining our already deep sense of tradition and fine technique with a feeling for modern needs. But in doing so, let us at the same time shun all eccentricities and select only those aspects of the modern masters that are suitable for the miniature's intimate and decorative functions. With intelligence and artistic sensibility, success will be achieved; with ignorance and reaction, nothing but failure will result.

The patron can help by being discriminating in his patronage and by encouraging the original miniaturist along his true paths. Also—and this is of prime importance—in encouraging the portrait miniaturist along the paths of true portraiture and sharply discouraging all flattery and pseudo-idealistic sentimentality. I know that this is asking much, especially if the patron wants to leave to future generations an untrue image of how he would prefer to appear; but, by insistence on artistic verity, he will be doing a great service to the art's future. In the case of artists like Lisa de Montfort, Joan Ayling, and Marjory Forbes, it is better to give the artist full rein, but in many other cases a more critical attitude would be of immensely greater value.

And lastly, the art critic might give more attention to the work of miniaturists. I strongly suspect that many of these experts either never go to an exhibition of miniatures or that if they do they merely glance around, notice some particularly blatant pieces of sentimentality, and go no deeper into the matter, leaving the sheep and goats as hopelessly mixed as before. At the present time the art critic enjoys more power than he has ever had before. His main task is to form public opinion and to advise the artist into which path he should direct his talents. If only every art critic in the country would devote but one article every twelve months to the subject of contemporary miniatures the result would be a general improvement in the standard of work done and a general awakening of public interest.

As was said at the beginning of this chapter, the available material is good and from the present roots much healthy growth can be induced. May all concerned take note and help to perpetuate this beautiful and fascinating art!

CHAPTER FIVE

Artistic Trends and Demands
of the Miniature

NOW that we have a general idea of the history of the English miniature in its most important phases, from the earliest times up to the present day, an assessment of its main demands upon its exponents can be made. These demands differ essentially from those of larger types of painting, or at least are differently accentuated. The miniature's functions are more purely decorative and more intimate than those of most large paintings. It sets out to do different things and therefore places its accents differently.

THE AIM OF THE PORTRAIT MINIATURE

What should a serious portrait miniature do? Primarily it should speak the truth about its subject's character and appearance; the men and women in miniature portraits should be real men and women, not fanciful interpretations of what they might have been like if they had been angels or fairies. Children should not be etherealized darlings, but real girls and boys, fond of playing, fond even of making themselves dirty. They should not be represented as winged cherubs, in which guise Andrew Plimer painted his daughter, Selina, but real people, as in the two charming miniatures of little girls attributed to Isaac Oliver (Plate VII). The character should, ideally, in all portrait miniatures, be as firmly and precisely stated as in Samuel Cooper's work. The works of Cosway and most of his contemporaries, for all their charm, miss this entirely, though they are highly decorative. The two greatest delineators of character in the whole history of English miniature painting are Samuel Cooper and John Smart, and it is the work of these artists that inevitably forms the yardstick by which character in portrait miniatures is to be judged.

All extravagant forms of portraiture, such as the painting of eyes divorced from their face, should be studiously avoided. Many eighteenth-century miniaturists painted their sitters' eyes for setting in jewellery—a pointless conceit, for one single eye, or, for that matter, a dozen eyes, can tell us nothing of a person's character. It is a precedent which the contemporary miniaturist does well to ignore. A portrait miniature should be a portrait; nothing less will suffice.

Yet a plain likeness is not enough. The miniature portrait should always call up the very personality and presence of the sitter. He who holds a portrait miniature in his hand should feel that the subject is actually with him as he looks at the likeness. This is one of the most important ways in which the miniature scores over the photograph. The photograph, mechanically produced, gives no more than a plain statement of apparent fact. The good miniature, on the other hand, gives *presence* as well as *likeness*, for the true artist can "read" his sitter's character and personality, and is able to capture them in the miniature for all the years to come; it is a likeness, but a personification also.

The portrait miniature's background is important; properly used it can add greatly to a work's decorative value. The backgrounds of most of the earliest portrait miniatures, in illuminated manuscripts, included such accessories as landscapes, furniture, and flowers. Later, during the time of Hilliard, the comparatively plain background was more popular; but in the seventeenth century the landscape background gained in popularity. The eighteenth-century miniaturists showed a preference for plain backgrounds once again, whilst in the nineteenth century subject matter was again introduced in more abundance, yet with less taste than ever before, as can be seen in a great deal of the work of Sir W. C. Ross. To-day the general tendency is once more in the direction of the plainer background, with a notable and successful exception in the case of Lisa de Montfort. But whatever its form, the background should never intrude. The most important thing in any portrait is the face, and a miniature that does not give it first place cannot be regarded seriously. A background, sound in conception and execution, can improve the decorative value of a miniature beyond belief; an ill-conceived background can entirely spoil what might have been a good work.

Intimacy, too, is an important requirement. A miniature should be painted with a feeling for its size and should on no account attempt the grandiose; that quality belongs to the domain of the large painting. It is

PLATE VII

Each 2⅛ × 1⅝ in.

ISAAC OLIVER
Two Little Girls, Aged Four and Five
Victoria & Albert Museum, P.145–1910, P.146–1910
Crown copyright.

an old heresy that the miniature should not suffer by being enlarged—a heresy first encouraged by what Horace Walpole said of Cooper's work in comparison with that of Vandyck (see page 32). Whilst what he said was true in fact, and in many ways was a compliment to Cooper's greatness, there is no justification in painting miniatures at all if they would look better and grander on a larger scale. If they are going to be small, then a small size should be the best size for their appearance.

VISUAL DISTORTION

One aspect of miniature painting that affects, indeed, all forms of painting, particularly at the present time, is visual distortion. This may be justifiable but it must be admitted that throughout the more recent history of miniature painting it has taken unjustifiable forms. No artist can help using distortion sometimes; did not Degas say: "You must give the idea of the true by means of the false in painting?" But at the same time the falsehood must justify itself. It may be used if the general design demands it, or if it is needed to emphasize one particular expression of, for example, the subject's personality. It should never be used, as it so often has been, for sugary and sentimental exaggeration. The miniature, by its very nature, may invite preciosity, but the good painter will always try to avoid it. Andrew Plimer was a great offender. He exaggerated most of his women's eyes to such an extent that they appear cow-like in many cases. There are cases in which such a distortion might be justified, but Plimer did it too often. He used distortion to exaggerate sentimentality in his sitters, and thus gave a falsified interpretation. It could be argued that his sitters were in reality sentimental, and in some cases this may certainly have been so; but it could not have been so in all, for character is not so stereotyped as that.

Do not misunderstand me. Any emotion is eligible for interpretation in painting, from fear to courage, from tears to laughter and from love to hate; even sentimentality may have its niche in the architecture of the art, but it should not be used *ad nauseam*. Any emotion becomes disgusting if we have too much of it, and this type of excess has been repeated far too often in miniature painting. To contemporary miniaturists there are so many other vistas open that it is unnecessary for them to try to emulate what artists like Plimer have already said only too forcibly. In judging the sentimental representations made by past miniaturists the critic should ask himself, before passing judgment, what was expected of the artist by his patrons in his own day. In other words, did he live at a time when sentimental idealizations were the fashion? If so, such idealizations are to some extent excusable, but only in artists of the second rank. The greater artist has always risen above questions of mere fashion to find other outlets for his creative skill, either in poetical and lyrical idealizations, as in the cases of Holbein and Hilliard, or in realism, as with Smart and Cooper. Such an artist can usually be assessed only on his own terms.

To sum up, the portrait miniature should achieve four main aims: (1) it should bring the very presence of the subject to the viewer; (2) it should portray an important part, or parts, of the sitter's character, or give an insight into his psychological make-up; (3) it should have decorative value; (4) it should be intimate in conception.

In the five centuries during which the art has been practised few miniatures have been produced which have held these four requirements in the nicest balance. The Elizabethans, for example, placed more accentuation on the third and fourth conditions than they did on the first two. On the other hand, Cooper accentuated the first and second, and in the eighteenth century the accent again shifted on to decoration and intimacy. Perhaps it would be asking too much of any artist to expect him consistently to bring them into the most refined balance. Hilliard did, in individual works (for instance in his "A Youth leaning against a Tree among Roses"); and so did Oliver, Cooper, Smart, and several others. But even amongst the greatest it was a balance evident in only a proportion of their total output. The ideal should be present just the same, however, and it should be the aim of every portrait miniaturist to achieve it. Amongst contemporaries, Lisa de Montfort comes nearest to a complete balance; but we really have no artist at the present time who can achieve it to anything like the extent of the old masters.

THE AIM OF THE SUBJECT MINIATURE

In the case of the subject miniature, decorative quality and gem-like depth of colour should *never* be absent, or it will, even more than the portrait miniature, be merely another small picture. In addition to this, the quality of intimacy is also a prime requirement. The subject miniature, quite as much as the portrait miniature, should be painted for examination by one person at one time; any miniature painted without this idea in the artist's mind is hardly worthy of the name. This was well known to the medieval illuminators, whose miniatures were, almost without exception, consciously addressed to the one person who would be reading the book. Although many miniatures of those days portrayed grand and stirring events, the quality of intimacy in the best of them was never absent.

Beyond the requirements of decoration and intimacy, there are few hard and fast rules that can be laid down to apply to all subject miniatures. Their aims are far more variable than those of portrait miniatures, but they are conditioned by what the individual work sets out to do. So far as style is concerned, the miniaturist may quite legitimately work in any he wishes, so long as he keeps within the demands of the art. So many self-styled miniaturists, especially at the present time, merely paint small pictures which they call miniatures, but from what has been said already in this book, it will be abundantly clear that they are nothing of the kind. They must have that extra jewel-like depth and that intense decorative quality. In fact, if it were not for this, many works by artists like Vuillard and Corot, to mention but two of many, would come into the category of miniature painting, which they most assuredly do not.

The general idea of the functions of a miniature in an illuminated manuscript has not altered much since the Middle Ages. In an illuminated book the miniature should be an accompaniment to, and an enrichment of, the calligraphy. It must be remembered that a book's main function is to be read, and for this reason alone the miniatures on its pages should be unobtrusively bound up with the lettering. That is why I feel that such miniatures should not, except in special cases, be illustrations in their own right, but should be dispersed amongst the text, as an enrichment to initial letters, as vignettes in borders, or as head- or tail-pieces. If the greatest care is used, full-page miniatures may also be used, but even they should run as a counterpoint to the lettering. In more realistic periods of the art, the realism of the miniature was often led up to from the calligraphy, by taking it one step from the writing, through a semi-realistic design of the surrounding border. The calligraphic miniature was at its best in the Celtic School, for every part of the decorations in manuscripts of that period was conceived and executed in a purely linear manner; from this point of view they doubtless served their purpose better than the miniatures of any other school. Whilst one can only admire the charm of the more realistic productions of the fourteenth and fifteenth centuries, there is little doubt that what went before was more suitable as an accompaniment to the texts. In many of the older manuscripts, text and miniatures were so closely bound up that one would seem lost without the other. This fact, in itself, justifies the transference of the illuminated full-page miniature to the frame for use as a devotional picture, or for purely ornamental purposes. So presented, its jewel-like qualities can be seen at their best without being hampered by, or hampering, a text. The realistic illuminated miniature, when it could no longer be justifiably contained in a book, followed this necessary and logical development.

An interesting class of subject-miniature painting is that which has grafted lessons taken from larger types of painting on to its own main traditions. Of course it is perfectly obvious that not all forms of large painting are of value to the miniaturist. The curious paintings that were produced from time to time by Paul Klee, for example, could be no use whatever to us, from either a technical or aesthetic viewpoint, because technically they belong to the kindergarten, and aesthetically they belong to the psychologist's clinic—neither of which are likely to yield anything of value to the decorative and jewel-like aims of the miniaturist.

On the other hand, painters of the stamp of Vuillard, Bonnard, and Matisse can exert an influence which is valuable for both reasons. To this group belongs the work of Marjorie Rodgers, who, as I have said before, shows strong signs of the influence of Léon Bakst; Kathleen Henderson and Lucy Pierce, who have used the English water-colour school for their purposes; Kathleen Goodman, who has assimilated a certain amount of Sargent's impressionism; and London Wood, who, in parts of his miniatures, uses an adaption of the pointillism of Pissaro; also such artists as Dulac, Rackham, Heath Robinson, and other illustrators, who are descended aesthetically from the illuminators and are really miniaturists but who belong to the indirect traditions of book-illustration.

To judge this type of subject miniature two questions should be asked. Firstly, is the borrowed development an enrichment to miniature painting, or is it just an oddity, foreign to the art and used merely for effect? Secondly, could the subject have been rendered better, or as well, by what the miniaturist has at his disposal in his own tradition already? If the art has indeed been enriched by the appropriation of lessons, either technical or aesthetic, from larger painting, and if the individual miniature could not have been painted so successfully without such appropriations then it is safe to say that they are justified, and the work may be judged as sound in these respects.

No cohesive school of miniature painting worthy of the name has yet been developed from the sources of large painting alone. How, indeed, could there be? Every art has its roots in its own traditions and wherever its branches may go these roots cannot be ignored, or a hybrid art will result, which will prove barren.

The last group of subject miniatures, copies of larger works, presents more difficulty for its justification than any of the others. The artistic justification of copies of works of art in any form is a moot point, but in adapting an idea from the terms of one medium into the terms of another a certain justification is apparent; for, in any case, what does an artist who paints from life do if he does not synthesize an image from one medium to another, from that of nature to that of paint? He is a creator none the less, because he re-creates the image in his own medium. So a copyist can to some extent be a creator, by transferring the image of a painting by another artist into his own terms and medium. It must in no circumstances be a plagiarism, however, but a creative transfer. This is the most difficult type of miniature to paint successfully. It takes an artist of the stature of, say, Peter Oliver to transfer a Titian to miniature size, without making it into a travesty. But to-day a copy of a larger picture, although it may not be of such a high artistic standard, has the special justification of suitability to cramped modern living conditions.

To sum up, the subject miniature must fulfil the requirements of (1) decorative value, (2) intimacy, and (3) the particular aims of its group, which may be either (a) in an illuminated manuscript, (b) an illuminated miniature painted for the frame, (c) the miniature from group (b) but enriched by aspects taken from larger painting, (d) copies of larger paintings.

As in the case of the portrait miniature, the requirements I have given are largely ideals and are intended as a criterion by which their quality may be judged. For my own part I know that I often violate them, for not every work may be judged by the same standard, but there must be ideal standards and I feel that the foregoing supply them. Other miniaturists and critics would doubtless disagree with details, but, taking a full historical view, they seem to be a common denominator for most of the best work. Occasionally a masterpiece has been produced which defies all standards, and such a work can only be judged on its own terms. You cannot judge a Cooper or an Oliver by a cross-section of the qualities of a hundred lesser men, but you can form a general idea of what is to be expected from any painter who practises the art.

CHAPTER SIX

Technique

TECHNIQUE in miniature painting is as varied as it is in large painting, and ranges from oil painting on the one hand to water-colour on the other, and from enamels to tempera. All are perfectly legitimate, so long as they are used in such a way as to meet the critical requirements mentioned in the last chapter. In the present chapter I wish to go quickly over the main tendencies in technique at the present time, and then to give some instructions on a typical method—one, in fact, that I use myself. This is the traditional method used up to the end of the art's heyday at the close of the eighteenth century, and of course the most commonly used to-day, for by far the greater number of miniaturists keep to it. There are many variations, from the style of direct painting of Alice Bingham to the highly polished and finely finished work of Mabel Rahbula and Isabel Saul; but all are really derived from the same source.

ALTERNATIVE METHODS

Oil painting is another traditional method that finds favour with such artists as Lisa de Montfort and Lieutenant-Colonel Goddard. This technique seems to be particularly favoured by the realists, and with good reason, for it is eminently suitable for strong light-and-shade contrasts, for natural colouring, and for its great adaptability. It is, however, a sticky medium to use for small work and requires considerable skill for painting on such a minute scale.

As mentioned in the last chapter, the technique of traditional English water-colour painting has been successfully adapted to miniature painting by such artists as Kathleen Henderson, Lucy Pierce, and others.

Enamel is a rare medium in this country to-day, but is used successfully for decorative purposes by a few artists. It is by far the most beautiful method so far as brilliance of colour is concerned, and has the advantage of absolute permanence, for the colours are fixed in place in an oven and no damage can come to such a work unless it is completely smashed. Sunlight, damp, and atmospheric conditions in general, have no effect upon its brilliance. The difficulties of the medium are manifold, but once mastered they offer lasting pleasure and give almost complete permanence to one's work. This book, however, is concerned with enamels only in so far as they affect the main stream of English miniature painting, and a detailed treatise on the technique would be beyond its scope. For those who wish to learn more about it I recommend a perusal of Millenet's book, mentioned in the Bibliography.

The contemporary school is fortunately free from the many freak techniques in evidence during past periods, which included such travesties as calligrams (i.e. "painting" in writing), "painting" in needlework and even in human hair; though it is certainly a pity that the beautiful églomisé process (see page 88) seems to have died out entirely.

PATIENCE ESSENTIAL

To come to the actual method of miniature painting, I must point out the paramount necessity for unlimited patience. This type of work cannot be carried out hurriedly, except by an occasional genius of Cosway's stamp, and genius though this artist certainly was, he could, by giving a little extra time to his work, have done even better work than he did. All the patience, care, and loving workmanship one can summon up must be bestowed upon these tiny paintings. For the beginner especially, impatience must be entirely repressed, for it will require a great deal of practice, accompanied by many disappointments, before any real skill can be developed. On no account should too much be attempted at one time. It will only lead to irritability and frustration, with the result that no work of any value will ever be produced.

Good results will come far more quickly to the artist who is content to practise for half an hour at a sitting without straining his eyes, and without growing tired. The golden rule, which I have learned from long experience, is to leave off when you feel you could go on for another hour. When I first began to paint miniatures I several times spoilt what promised to be good work by carrying on just a little too long in my excitement. Now I rarely paint for longer than an hour at a time.

THE IMPORTANCE OF CLEANLINESS

Of equal importance is the cultivation of complete cleanliness in one's method of work. It is essential that, as far as possible, all dust should be excluded from the room in which one is working, and half an hour spent in dusting and cleaning the room before beginning work each time will be well rewarded. Dust will spoil many larger paintings, and a speck of dust appears so big in a smaller work that it can ruin it completely. Hilliard, in his *Treatise Concerning the Arte of Limning*, is most emphatic about it, and says: "Them the fierst and cheefest precepts which I giue is cleanlynes, and therfor fittest for gentlemen, that the practicer of limning be presizly pure and klenly in all his doings, as in grinding his coulers in place wher ther is neither dust nor smoake, the watter wel chossen or distilled most pure, as the watter distilled from the watter of some clear spring, or frome black cherize, which is the cleanest that euer I could find, and keepeth longest sweet and cleare . . . at the least let your aparell be silke, such as sheadeth lest dust [*sic*] or haires, weare nothing straight, beware you tuch not your worke with your fingers, or any hard thing, but with a cleane pencel brush it, or with a whit feather, neither breathe one it, especially in could weather, take heed of the dandrawe [*dandruff*] of the head sheading from the haire, and of speaking ouer your worke for sparkling, for the least sparkling of spettel will neuer be holpen if it light on the face or any part of the naked." This advice may seem fastidious to a modern reader, but every word is justified, and if the miniaturist follows it implicitly he will have little cause to fear that his work may be spoiled by dust. The obvious way to overcome the problem of finding "silke aparell" in modern conditions is to wear a silk dressing-gown—a common enough piece of clothing.

UNDERSTANDING THE TRADITIONS OF THE ART

A usual mistake amongst beginners in any art is to learn its technique, without at the same time becoming acquainted with its traditions and aesthetics. Neither is this shortcoming confined to beginners; many contemporary miniaturists could improve their work a good deal if they knew more of its history and requirements. It is most important for the miniaturist to feed his mind, and this can best be done by diligent reading of books on the subject and frequent visits to museums and art galleries where such work is exhibited. Although in recent years few books have been published on the subject there were many such works put on the market in the first quarter of the present century; these can usually be picked up second-hand at prices ranging from a few shillings to a number of pounds. A glance at the Bibliography will give some idea of what is procurable. A study of the miniatures in the museums and art galleries can give practical insight into the aesthetic aims and principles of artists of the past, and much can be learnt in this way. But the artist, especially the novice, should guard against plagiarizing what he sees there. It is quite an easy matter to develop a facility for copying these works stroke for stroke, and whilst this may have its values from the point of view of pure practice it is dangerous ground to tread. Rather use what you see there to provide impetus for your own creative ideas. Profit by the lessons of the past, but keep their influence in check. It is always a good thing, too, to have a few original miniatures in your possession, thus giving your everyday life a valuable cultural background. Old miniatures may be purchased quite cheaply in antique shops and at auctions, and modern examples can be bought just as cheaply, whilst initials and miniatures from old illuminated manuscripts may be sometimes picked up for as little as a few shillings each from antiquarian book-sellers and curio shops. If it is impossible for you to buy originals, then the Victoria and Albert Museum, the Wallace Collection, and many other such institutions, supply excellent photographs of many of the works in their various collections at prices ranging from a few pence each.

On no account should the miniaturist practise by sketching, for this will give him an excessive tendency to looseness and coarseness, whereas his main aim should be compactness and finish—at least in his early stages. Miniature painting is a meticulous art and makes great demands on its exponents; it calls for the highest refinement and the strongest linear qualities. Sketching may have its virtues in relation to other forms of painting (though even this is questionable) but in miniature painting it is a dangerous waste of time. Rather should the miniaturist train his memory to note what his eye sees; this should then be put into paint in the more tranquil atmosphere of his studio. This method was used by many of the European old masters, and has been used for centuries by Oriental artists; it gives the artist time to assimilate his subject and to interpret it at leisure. Sketching, on the other hand, encourages a slavish copying of fleeting impressions, instead of that deeper insight which is the core of all sound painting.

MATERIALS REQUIRED

Materials for miniature painting are, in common with those of other arts, in short supply at present. The situation with regard to some of these is certainly easier now, but it will be years before supplies are really normal once again. With this in mind, I have in many cases indicated substitutes in the pages that follow: I have used them all myself and so can recommend them with confidence. In any case, it is often as well for the beginner to use substitutes, for not only will he find most of them more economical to use than the real things, which are often very expensive, but also he will not be denying them to finished professional artists to whom they represent a means of livelihood.

Until the seventeenth century, vellum or parchment were by far the commonest materials on which miniatures were painted, although Pliny says that ivory was first used as a painting surface by one Jaja of Cyzieus as early as 50 B.C. Actually, so far as miniatures are concerned, its first use is usually attributed to Bernard Lens. To-day we have the choice of either, and which is to be used depends largely upon the artist's individual aims and technique. The surface if ivory would be wasted upon a body-colour technique, but comes into its own when a wash technique is employed. Generally speaking, portraits are more successful upon ivory, as it imparts a delicate and quick lustre to the skin, and with imagination the grain of its surface may be incorporated into the general design. Katherine Henderson is particularly happy in doing this in her landscapes, allowing the grain of the ivory to follow the contours of the hills and undulations of the fields. Vellum is a delightful ground for the reception of body-colour, and has a smooth velvety feeling which reacts pleasantly upon the brush. It is much cheaper than ivory, but in many ways is more difficult to use, owing to its greasy nature; once mastered, however, it is, in my opinion, the pleasanter of the two from the artist's point of view. I use both, and have found that with discrimination they are both invaluable in their respective applications. There are many grades and thicknesses of vellum, from fine Roman (lambskin) to the coarsest goatskin. Each grade has its uses, which the miniaturist will discover with experience, and each has a latent wealth of possibilities. Parchment is not so good because it turns yellow in time, but is cheaper and quite good for the beginner to practise upon. He would be well advised, however, to use neither parchment, vellum, nor ivory until he has to some extent mastered his brushwork, for all are at least fairly expensive and merit use only in works of some permanent aesthetic value. For his purpose I recommend Bristol board, or very fine handmade paper of sufficient thickness for it not to cockle when the paint is applied.

THE PRELIMINARY DRAWING

Having selected a material to work upon, the next step is to make the preliminary drawing on a piece of smooth paper, stout enough to withstand the inevitable rubbing-out. The main reason for making this separate drawing is that if any alterations are necessary it will not matter so much if the paper is smudged as it would on the actual miniature, for however thoroughly the smudges are cleaned a small amount of graphite will always remain embedded in its surface, sooner or later causing discoloration of the paint. An HB grade pencil will be found best for the preliminary drawing, as it gives a dark enough impression without undue pressure, which might cramp freedom of movement. The design itself should be neat, flowing, and free, but the essential feeling for intimacy should not be absent. It cannot be stressed too strongly that anything grandiose is absolutely foreign to the miniature's nature. Do not leave the preliminary drawing until you are perfectly satisfied that it is the best you can do, for it will be the very foundation of your work. A little extra trouble at this early stage will make all the difference to the finished work, but do not expect in the first place to design work that will compare with that of such finished artists as Albert Cousins, Lisa de Montfort, and Joan Ayling; that will only come, if at all, with continual hard work. You must be the judge of what is your best, but do not be too hard upon yourself.

In portraits, the placing of the head is an important factor. It should be well placed in the shape of your miniature (ovals, by the way, are generally better for portraits as they follow the shape of the head). No strict rule can be made for this, as every head needs slightly different placing according to its shape and expression, and according to the subject's personality. A study of Cosway's work will yield much interesting information regarding the placing of heads.

In subject miniatures, the main objects of interest should be worked into the design in such a way that the subsidiary objects radiate or recede from them, more or less unobtrusively, according to their importance to the design. Colour, it is true, can help greatly here, but the design itself is the basis of everything that follows, and the miniaturist should rely upon it in the first place. A good check on the success of a design is to hold the miniature upside-down, and if the main objects still stand out, and the design still appears as a cohesive whole without patchiness, it may be adjudged a success. Even the almost unbelievably complicated designs of the Celtic illuminators will stand up to this test completely satisfactorily. Above all, do not overcrowd your miniature. Bear in mind that it is a tiny work of but a few square inches at most and cannot contain the profusion of, for example, a Breughel crowd scene.

TRANSFERRING THE DESIGN

The preliminary drawing being finished, the next thing to do is to get it transferred to your working surface. If paper, Bristol board, parchment, or vellum are being used, one of two methods may be employed: either by using a stylus (a pointed instrument set in a handle), or by squaring up your original drawing and transferring it square by square. It is as well to practise in both methods and find out by experience which suits you better. If the former method is used the material you are using for your finished miniature should be fixed beneath the preliminary drawing by means of drawing pins, and all the lines of the design should be firmly traced over with the stylus. Upon removal of the original, an indented impression will be found beneath. This method has the advantage that no graphite is likely to become embedded in the miniature, but it has the obvious drawback that once the lines have been indented, there can be no alteration without the indentations showing up. If the second method is used, the original is squared up, as in Plate VIII, and a corresponding number of squares are marked off on the material of the miniature itself. The design is then transferred square by square. This method has the drawbacks of the use of pencil on the finished work, with its accompanying risk of embedded graphite and subsequent discoloration, and secondly of the difficulty in maintaining spontaneity of line in a transferred drawing. But it has the advantage of allowing alterations to be made with greater facility, and also that it enables you to see the results of your work whilst you are doing it.

When the design has been transferred, trace over the pencil or incised lines with vandyke brown, using a fine sable brush, afterwards carefully rubbing away any superfluous pencil-marks. The next step is lightly to pounce the miniature. This process has been in use for centuries and consists of rubbing a small amount of powder (made from an equal mixture of french chalk and powdered pumice) all over the surface with a small piece of chamois leather or some similar material. The idea is to remove any greasy or shiny patches from the surface of the material on which you are working, as these would prevent the paint from "taking." A few seconds' rubbing is usually sufficient, although in the case of very greasy vellum as many minutes may be found necessary; the miniature is then thoroughly wiped over with a clean silk handkerchief, and particular care must be taken to ensure that every scrap of the powder has been removed, or it will mix with the paint with detrimental results. If vellum or parchment are being used it will be a good plan to pounce it thoroughly before doing any actual work on it at all, as these materials harbour a great deal of natural grease on their surfaces. Vellum, moreover, unless it is of a very thick grade, should be attached to a piece of card by means of white paste of the best quality. It is important to keep the vellum flat whilst doing this, or it may cockle, and once it has cockled no power on earth will induce it to go flat again. A good way to make sure that the flatness will be maintained is to put the vellum and card into a letter-press, tie-press, or trouser-press, until the paste is dry. If no such press is available the materials may be put between the leaves of a book with a weight over it. Always put the card and vellum between two sheets of clean white paper to dry, as this prevents them from picking up dust or becoming discoloured in some other way. And always use the best quality white paste as it is less likely to discolour the vellum than the cheaper kinds. Some firms undertake the mounting of vellum on card, but in my opinion the best way to become thoroughly acquainted with the technique of an art is to do as many of these things for yourself as you can.

Ivory may be purchased in a fairly large range of stock sizes from most good art material dealers. There are two main kinds, bleached and un-bleached. It is best to buy the unbleached variety and to treat it for yourself, as commercial bleaching is often carried out artificially with chemicals, which usually tend to discolour the paint after a time. Ivory may be bleached by dipping the leaf (as a piece of prepared ivory is called) into water, and placing it in the sun to dry, care being taken, however, that it is not left there long enough to curl and perhaps crack.

The leaf should be pounced before use, and held on to the drawing-board by means of small pins wedged against its sides. It is a good plan, in doing this, to leave one side absolutely free, so that the handling of the brushes is in no way interrupted. The transfer of the preliminary drawing to the ivory is much simpler than in the case of the other materials. All that is necessary is to slip the former beneath the leaf, and trace the lines straight on to the ivory with a brush. If the pencil lines do not show themselves up strongly enough through the ivory, the preliminary drawing may be drawn over in Indian ink, which will show up much better.

CHOICE OF PAINTS

To come to the choice of paints, only the very finest are suitable for miniature painting, as the cheaper kinds are often gritty or lumpy. Even the beginner should endeavour to buy only the best pigments. He should be able to afford to do this, for an ordinary tube of colour should last the average miniaturist many years. I have some which I purchased as long ago as 1937, and even now they have plenty of paint left in them. And, apart from these economical considerations, there is nothing worse for the beginner than to have to grapple with the added difficulty of colours that have nasty lumps in every brushful. If you ever do encounter lumpiness, it is as well to know how to overcome it. The materials necessary for this are two pieces of plate glass, one about ten inches square, and the other in the form of a circle of about three inches diameter. The gritty paint is dropped on to the larger slab with a spot of ox-gall to prevent its becoming too dry, and is then ground beneath the circular slab until the paint is smooth enough to use. A palette knife is useful for gathering up the paint afterwards. Always clean the slabs with scrupulous care before grinding a second colour. On no account use pans or cakes of colour as they become dusty, even when closed down in a box. Tubes of ready-mixed colour, or powder with which you can mix your own colours, are the best, as you need take only just enough for your immediate requirements.

You will need a palette of some kind on which to prepare your paint, and some manufacturers make a white plastic palette which is eminently suitable; or, if you prefer to spend more money and have something even better, an ivory-cutter would make one up for you in that material. Andrew Plimer's palette was made of mother-of-pearl and that, too, is a good material, but oyster-shells are just as good—and much cheaper! Any of the china slants or saucers manufactured for water-colour painters are suitable, or an ordinary household saucer may be used with equal success. Enamelled tin is unsuitable, being likely to chip. Always clean your palette thoroughly. If you leave your paints on it you will find dust adhering to them when you come to use them again, and they will be useless in that state.

It would be ridiculous to lay down any set rules as to which particular colours are to be used, for so much depends upon what the individual artist has to express, but generally speaking it is best to keep your colours to the primary groups (i.e. reds, blues, and yellows) and to use only permanent ones. Some of the more fugitive tints give very beautiful effects when they are first applied, but such effects are ephemeral, and what is the use of going to endless trouble with a work that is destined to last perhaps a year or two at most? It is surely much better to keep to the more reliable colours and thus to ensure a degree of permanency for one's work. There are few things more discouraging to an artist than to see one of his works when it has faded into a mere shade of its original self. Most manufacturers supply lists of recommended permanent colours, and the intending miniaturist would be well advised to obtain one of these before choosing his range.

Personally I find that a group of about twelve colours is all that I require, and I have been able to paint many subjects with them, including even the plumage of that gorgeous bird, the peacock. Every miniaturist should try to develop his own colour harmonies, but for the sake of interest I will give a list of those pigments which I find most useful. They are: alizarin carmine, rose madder, Indian red, lemon yellow, aureolin, cobalt blue, ultramarine, cerulean blue, and vandyke brown.

PLATE VIII

RAYMOND LISTER, R.M.S., F.R.S.A.
Preliminary Drawing "Squared" for Transfer,
Preliminary Colour Sketch, and Finished
Miniature, Cocodrillo

BRUSHES

Next we come to the question of brushes, and here again only the best sables should be used. Cheap brushes are inclined to shed their hairs, causing endless trouble and vexation, and after all they are not so very much cheaper than good grades. The miniaturist naturally requires smaller brushes than the average painter, and unfortunately the smallest stock size at present is No. 00. It is possible to get the smaller grades (000 and 0000) made up specially, but naturally this is expensive. A good substitute is the pin-feather of the wood-cock which, with its shaft glued into an old brush-handle and its end barbs used for painting, is capable of painting the finest lines. Such feathers may be obtained from gamekeepers and game-dealers, who used to sell them to miniaturists in bygone days for as much as half-a-crown apiece, but who would probably make no charge for them to-day. No. 00 is the most generally useful of all sizes of brush to the miniaturist, but smaller ones are indispensable for stippling and dotting whilst larger ones are useful for broader washes.

The miniaturist should remember that his brushes are his main working tools, and he should, therefore, exercise the greatest care in keeping them in the best possible condition. Always clean them thoroughly after use, and store them in a tightly closed box, standing the box on its end so that the points of the brushes are not damaged.

APPLYING THE PAINT

There are various methods of applying the paint, in the form of dots, hatchings, or strokes of varying size. The older form of application, used in the days of illuminated manuscripts by Hilliard, Oliver, and their followers, was a fine stipple. Some illuminators, like Matthew Paris, used a wash and line technique, whilst Cosway, and many later miniaturists, used a looser adaptation of a combination of the earlier examples. All these techniques are in use to-day, and many others as well; but there is no doubt that it is best for the beginner to be thoroughly acquainted in the first place with the finest possible stippling. Firstly, when mastered, it gives a sound foundation to one's technique and one from which any other road may be taken; secondly, although some of the other methods appear easy they are not so in reality, being full of unlooked-for pitfalls for the inexperienced artist.

Mixtures of colour may be obtained by painting dots of primary colours in juxtaposition to each other on the miniature. For example, a dark green can be made by placing dots of ultramarine and lemon yellow side by side. Or they may be made by painting a wash of one primary colour over another. Orange may be made by painting a wash of alizarin carmine over one of aureolin. Of course the colours may be mixed before application, but this is inclined to detract from their brilliance, whereas the foregoing methods, especially the first mentioned, lose little or nothing in this respect.

It will be found useful to make a rough colour-sketch of the miniature before actually beginning work on the finished piece. This enables the artist to work out his colour scheme in a methodical way. Such a sketch is illustrated here by way of example (Plate VIII).

COLOURING PORTRAIT MINIATURES

The colouring of portrait miniatures requires a special note. The colours I give for this branch of the art are in no way intended as the only possible ones that can be used. The colours of individual complexions vary so much that at best they must be regarded as merely general indications.

The outlines are transferred in the normal way to the miniature's surface, but Indian red will be found more useful than vandyke brown in the case of portraits. The main areas of light and shade are then filled in, the thinnest washes of cobalt blue being used for the latter and of Indian red for the former. More detail may then be introduced, aureolin and rose madder being used for the main flesh colours. If ivory is being used, it may be left bare for highlights. Vermilion, toned down with rose madder, may be used for painting in the lips and the bloom of the cheeks. The portrait is finished off by hatching or stippling with the same colours.

THE USE OF GOLD

The early illuminators, followed by Hilliard and the Olivers, used shell gold for highlights on clothing and other objects, and for depicting jewellery. It may be so used at the present time, but care should be taken not to overdo it or the result will be too bizarre. Use as little of this material as possible.

Shell-gold is now unobtainable in the shops and I will therefore give a recipe for its preparation. Take half a dozen leaves of gold leaf and grind it to a fine powder between the two pieces of plate glass described on page 81, adding a few drops of clear honey and a little ox-gall. Do not allow the mixture to become too moist or too dry; the right consistency is that of a thin paste. A little extra ox-gall will thin down the mixture, and a little extra honey will thicken it. When the gold has been powdered as finely as possible and the whole mixed thoroughly together, it may be taken up from the glass on a palette knife and placed in an oyster- or mussel-shell for use. Keep the shell in an air-tight box to keep away the dust.

Shell silver may be similarly prepared, but I do not recommend it since it turns a dirty greyish-black in time. Some of the finest Elizabethan miniatures have been spoilt in this way, and where they once sparkled with silver, black blotches remain.

The method of application of these metallic paints is by dotting or stippling. If they are brushed on too boldly they will thin out and lose all their lustre. They should be applied after all the other painting has been completed, as otherwise they are liable to get into the other colours, giving them an unwanted sparkling effect.

Gold leaf may also be used for special effects, but its use should be even more sparing than that of shell-gold. I do not intend to go fully into the subject of gilding here, as its use is very limited in ordinary miniature painting, and it properly belongs to the sphere of the illuminator. Any good manual on the latter art will give full instructions. But I will give one important piece of advice, which is to apply gold leaf *before* the application of the paint; this is because the paint would stand the risk of being scratched when the gold is burnished.

FRAMING

The all-important subject of framing must be mentioned. Without doubt the best type of frame for a miniature is the small metal rim fitted with a convex glass. These are easier to obtain now than they have been for some time past, but it should be remembered that they are made in stock sizes, and unless you are prepared to spend a lot of money in having them specially made, you should obtain a list of available sizes so that you may paint your miniatures accordingly. Most framers will make up quite good little wooden frames to any reasonable size and shape, and for certain types of miniature these are more suitable and are, moreover, much cheaper than the metal ones.

Whatever type of frame you eventually choose for your work always remember that simplicity should be the keynote. On no account should deep frames be used as they throw shadows on to the miniatures they house; no picture can stand much of such shadow, let alone such small works as miniatures. And avoid antique frames unless there is some justification for it. To the experienced eye a modern picture in an antique frame is completely incongruous, charming though the superficial appearance many be.

FACTS TO REMEMBER

To the intending miniaturist I will offer a few final words of advice. First master your technique, and when you have mastered it remain its master. Do not make it an end in itself, but use it for what it is—a medium through which to express your own artistic ideals. Do not paint like a camera, but be original and do not be afraid to experiment. Our greatest need to-day is for original miniaturists with the courage of their own convictions. Photographic painting is dead, and it is the original miniaturists whose work will survive. Remember that you are a part of the art—it is not a part of you; to get the best out of it, you must put something of yourself into it. If you bear these simple facts in mind, you may well produce work of value that will survive for posterity.

CHAPTER SEVEN

Silhouettes

N O treatise on the art of miniature painting would be complete
without some reference to the closely related art of the silhouette,
more correctly called the shade or profile. Just as in miniature
painting proper England occupies a position in the front rank, so has she
done in the art of the silhouette. In fact it is true to say that our noble tradition
in the former has made our achievements in the latter more pronounced.
Some of our great silhouettists have been pupils of well-known miniaturists,
an especial example being Mrs. Beetham, who was a pupil of John Smart.
More will be said of her work later.

THE DEVELOPMENT OF THE ART

The art itself is of great antiquity. A story from Pliny says that it originated
about six centuries before Christ, when Korinthea, daughter of Dibutades
a potter, traced the shadow of her lover's profile when he was taking farewell
of her. Pleasant though this story is, we need more corroborative evidence
before it can be called anything but apocryphal. Some have sought to trace
its origin in the black figures and heads to be seen on Greek vases, and
although there may be an element of truth in this the same cautious scepticism
must be preserved. Profiles of various subjects, as distinct from portraits,
were known in the Middle Ages and were quite popular in Tudor times.
Origins may also be sought in the ancient shadow-puppets of the East.
A guild of paper-cutters certainly existed in the Near East at an early date,
and it may well be that the embryo of the art is to be sought here. Shadow-
theatres were in use in Mohammedan countries as early as the seventh century.
Although the shadow portrait is named after Etienne de Silhouette, Controller-
general of finance in France under Louis XV, he was not in fact its originator,
although he worked in the medium as an amateur. The reason why his name
is so closely associated with it is that it was in the first place a cheap
substitute for the miniature proper and Silhouette had, because of the taxes

inflicted by him upon the *noblesse* during his tenure of office, earned a reputation as the cause of such things.

The shadow portrait that is familiar to us to-day first became popular in the middle of the eighteenth century. From this time until the advent of the daguerreotype both professional and amateur profilists were at work in vast numbers, whilst even to-day a few artists work in the medium. The art of silhouette-cutting must indeed have been as popular a pastime in the reign of George III as is that of taking snapshots to-day. The Royal Court took to the art, and soon many of its members were enthusiastically cutting one another's likenesses; George's daughter, Princess Elizabeth, was one of the most accomplished of these amateurs.

There are several processes which have been employed from time to time, probably the earliest of which is the cut-paper process, in which the artist worked free-hand with no other implement than a pair of scissors (some of the greatest profilists used this method). There were also many mechanical devices. One favourite method was that known as the églomisé process, in which the profile was painted in reverse on the back of a glass, and usually backed with some coloured paper or tin-foil. This process was named after Jean Baptiste Glomi (*circa* 1760), who, although he made use of it, was not really its inventor. Yet another method was to paint the shadow on to slabs of plaster in an intense black pigment, such as Indian ink or a preparation of tallow smoke. A variation of the églomisé process was to paint the portrait in reverse on the back of a convex glass, the back being filled in with either coloured pigment or wax. But perhaps the most beautiful results are to be obtained by simply painting the shade on ivory, vellum, card, or paper. Although silhouettes are occasionally found on porcelain, particularly Royal Worcester Ware, they are very rarely to be seen in enamel.

Apart from its straightforward use for portraits and other kinds of pictures, the applications of the shade were many. Tobacco-boxes, snuff-boxes, patch-boxes, card-boxes—even perfume-bottle stoppers are to be found with profiles worked into their decorative pattern. In jewellery they are frequently seen on rings and bracelets, and seals were sometimes made to open and reveal a profile inside them. Until comparatively recent times it was common for a small sum to be bequeathed in wills for the purchase of mourning rings as keep-sakes, and shades of the departed were commonly incorporated in such rings. Shades are also to be found on drinking-glasses, goblets, salt-cellars, and many other forms of household utensils. A *millefleur* paper-weight is known which contains no less than twenty-two silhouettes of Queen Victoria. The famous French miniaturist, Isabey, painted glass buttons with portraits, flowers, and other subjects, and in this direction too, the profile subsequently made its appearance. The fashion extended to personal stationery; silhouettes were used to grace mourning-cards, and in lighter vein, valentines; whilst visiting-cards were often printed with a fashionably attired lady or gentleman in profile in one corner.

THE CONVERSATION GROUP

One popular form of the silhouette was the conversation or family group, which first became popular during the earlier part of the eighteenth century. One of the best exponents of this kind of silhouette to practise in this country was Francis Torond (1743–1812), a French refugee who worked at Bath and later in London. His real name is unknown, the one he used being a pseudonym. The work produced by him is of great beauty and makes one grieve that it is so rare. These shades take us into the intimate family lives of the people he portrayed, either gathered around the table at a meal, sipping coffee, or engaged in needle-work, reading, and other such occupations.

Another exponent of the conversational shade was A. Charles, who also painted miniatures, but his efforts in the latter form are very poor compared with his silhouettes (Plate LXI). He worked towards the end of the eighteenth century and was one of the very few silhouettists whose trade labels mentioned work in enamel, as well as the more usual processes. His office was opposite the Lyceum in the Strand, and at first his prices for shades varied from half a crown to four guineas. But upon being appointed painter of likenesses to the Prince of Wales in 1793, he raised his prices considerably and his cheapest figure was then half a guinea. Of excellent quality, his work stands in the front rank of that of English profilists.

FAMOUS PROFILISTS

The most important branch of work in this medium is the familiar shade portrait which assumed many forms, from severe black-and-white to gilded and coloured examples. Isabella Beetham was one of the great figures in this type of portrait (Plate LXI). In fact she was described thus in Mrs. Jackson's book, *Silhouette:* "She is the Holbein amongst shadow-painters in that she can give elaborate detail in dress without weakening the interest in the face." One can but concur in the opinion that she was a fine profilist, but to couple her name with one so illustrious as the great sixteenth-century artist is rather fanciful. Having run away from home at the age of twenty, Isabella Robinson met Edward Beetham, the son of a Westmorland man of means, and they fell in love and were married. At first they were in financially difficult circumstances, but Isabella found that she had a talent for cutting profile portraits and applied herself to it with some energy. She was encouraged in this by Foote, the actor, and at last decided to turn professional. Having had a measure of success with some inventions, her husband bought the lease of a property in Fleet Street in 1782, where his wife set up her studio. She soon decided to abandon the cutting method, and took lessons from John Smart the miniaturist, upon whose style she based her own. She certainly executed ordinary miniatures, for one at least from her hand is known which is obviously not the work of a novice. Her husband died in 1809, after founding the Eagle Assurance Office together with Sir William Rawlings, and after this date little further is known of her. Her portrait was painted by Gainsborough in 1784, but unfortunately has since been destroyed. Mrs. Beetham did a certain amount of work for use in jewellery, to which her very fine and polished technique lent itself admirably.

Bath being a great centre of fashion in the eighteenth century, it is little wonder that many portrait painters and profilists had their studios in that town. Hamlet, the profilist, rented a studio in the same street as that of Gainsborough. This artist painted miniatures, but is best known for his silhouettes painted on glass (Plate LXII). His work is mostly full-length and he often used gold foil to ornament it. He was evidently a fast worker, for one of his advertisements stated that he could take a striking likeness in one minute for half a crown!

Major John André (Plate LXII), who was born in Geneva in 1751, must also be mentioned. He came to England, joined the army and was sent to fight in America. He at first made a great success of his military career and was appointed aide-de-camp, first to General Grey, and then to Sir Henry Clinton.

Unfortunately for him he was entrusted with important negotiations with the notorious Benedict Arnold who was planning a betrayal to the English. The unfortunate Major was captured, and in spite of his personal messages to General Washington, asking to be allowed to die a soldier's death, was hanged as a spy in 1780. There is a monument to his memory in Westminster Abbey. Although an amateur cutter of shades, his work would have done credit to many professionals, and had it not been for his military career he could doubtless have spent much more time upon it than he actually found possible, in which case he would have taken a foremost place, even amongst the great silhouettists who were his contemporaries.

One of the greater figures amongst profilists was John Miers, who was born in 1758 and died in 1821, his life thus spanning the art's most flourishing period. He was named after his father, who was a native of Leeds and a painter, though whether a painter of pictures or a household decorator we do not know. John Miers travelled widely in the north of England, but settled in London in 1788, where he took John Field, who was himself to become a well-known silhouettist, into his employment as an assistant and later as a partner. Miers's work is noted for its excellent representations of character, and in this he remains unequalled. He painted his silhouettes on card or plaster.

An original worker of the time, although one can hardly call his work beautiful, was the Swedish-born profilist, W. A. Spornberg, who practised at Bath towards the end of the eighteenth century (Plate LXVII). This artist's method was a complete reversal of the usual one inasmuch as he left the profile itself untouched, except for a few suggestions for eyes, mouth, and other features, and painted the background black, surrounding the head with designs resembling Greek key patterns. He painted on the back of convex glass, and usually painted in the profile and pattern with red pigment. Although his work is very rare, and collectors pay large prices for it, there is no doubt that it is not silhouette work in the strictest sense; it resembles beer labels as much as anything!

In this connexion it is interesting to see what the eighteenth-century writer P. H. Perrehon, writes in his *A Detailed Treatise of Silhouettes*, on a process similar to that used by Spornberg. He says: "The glass must be cleaned with powdered chalk to remove all grease and dirt, then cover one side with fine ground white lead mixed with gum water. When this is dry take the profile cut out of strong paper, lay it on the glass, trace round it the outline of the portrait, with a needle. Scrape away all the white within the drawing; transparency is thus obtained. It may be made black by laying on a piece of black velvet, cloth, paper, or taffeta. One can stick on the paper cutting, using the gum to cover the white ground as well, or one can put foil, gold, or silver." Spornberg's method was similar to this except, of course, that he used a black composition instead of the white lead alluded to above. The details in the face he would probably have scraped on with some kind of needle.

One of the silhouette's most notable characters was Edward Ward Foster, who was born in 1761 of wealthy parents (Plate LXIII). This artist was a miniature-painter to Queen Charlotte and Princess Amelia. He was one of the first to discard the plain black-and-white silhouette and to use colour and gold. It seems that he was afraid of no experiment in this direction, and if one does occasionally lament the results he is at least to be admired as a pioneer. His fame is further enhanced by the fact that he died in 1865 at the age of 103, after marrying five times.

Mrs. Sarah Harrington was a profilist having the same general conceptions of the art as Spornberg, in that her portraits were white with black backgrounds (Plate LXVI). In her case, however, the results were much happier. She worked in the last quarter of the eighteenth century and had a studio in New Bond Street, London. Her portraits were cut in white paper which she placed on to another sheet of black paper or material, and although she used machinery (it is known that she applied for a patent for her profile-cutting machine) her work rarely shows the stiffness usually associated with this type of cutting.

MECHANICAL METHODS

In speaking of mechanical methods, a case may be recalled in which an automaton was used as a form of trickery at a somewhat later date than this. A contemporary advertisement ran as follows—

"Now Exhibiting in apartments over the shop of Mr. Liddell, show maker, corner of the Market Place, Huddersfield, PROSOPGRAPHUS, the Automaton Artist. This splendid little figure possesses the extraordinary power of drawing by mechanical means, the Likeness of any Person, that is placed before it, in the short space of One Minute. It is hoped that the Inhabitants of Huddersfield, will come forward with their usual spirit, to encourage a piece of ingenuity at once novel and curious. A likeness in Black for one shilling. Coloured from 7. 6. upwards. Open from Ten till Eight."

A later writer in *Notes and Queries* had the following to say regarding the remarkable claims of this machine: "I remember very well the automaton which professed to draw Silhouettes. Somewhere about 1826 the automaton was brought to Newcastle. It was a figure seated in flowing robes, with a style in the right hand, which by machinery scraped an outline of a profile on a card which the exhibitor professed to fill up in black. The person whose likeness was to be taken sat at one side of the figure near a wall. One of our party detected an opening in the wall through which a man's eye was visible. This man, no doubt, drew the profile, and not the automaton. Ladies' heads were relieved by pencillings in gold. Another performer, I remember, went to work in a more scientific manner; a long rod, worked in a movable fulcrum, with a pencil at one end and a small iron rod at the other, was his apparatus. He passed the rod over the face and head, and the pencil at the other end reproduced the outline on a card, afterwards filled in with lampblack."

THE USE OF COLOUR

It is obvious, when an art has to revert in this way to trickery and mechanical methods, that it is on the wane; and by this time it certainly seemed that its true place was on the fairground or market-place, rather than in the studios of respected artists like Miers and Mrs. Beetham. Nor was this the only sign of degeneracy, for whatever may have been the charm of coloured profiles, and it must be admitted that many of these had beauty almost in spite of themselves, they do not rival the classical simplicity of the pure black-and-white silhouette. From the time of Foster onwards there had been an increasing tendency to use colour, first in simple and unobtrusive forms, such as the indication of hair by gold, or clothes by colour; and later by more fantastic methods of painting the face green or red and indicating the rest of the portrait in natural colours. Such work could hardly be called shades with any degree of accuracy.

Notable exceptions to the many fantastic colour schemes are to be found in the work of J. Buncombe. This profilist's excellent representations of soldiers from many regiments, their faces in dead black, but attired in gaily coloured uniforms correct in every detail, are unequalled (Plates LXIII, LXIV). Working from about 1775 to 1825 at Newport, Isle of Wight, Buncombe had every opportunity of studying accoutrements, for many regiments visited the Isle. Apart from their intrinsic artistic merit his silhouettes are of great value to students of the history of military equipage, being in some cases the only records in existence of certain uniforms. No inaccuracies in the details of the uniforms have ever been detected. Buncombe's profiles are extremely rare, and the collector must beware particularly of reproductions cut from art magazines, and framed to be sold as originals. Many particularly clever fakes have been made in France, but these are easily distinguishable as they are invariably painted on ivory, and Buncombe did not use this material at all.

THE FINAL PERIOD OF GREATNESS

There is no doubt that so far as coloured profiles are concerned Buncombe's work stands in a class of its own, and the many monstrosities produced in colour during the first quarter of the nineteenth century brought the art to a really low level. It was rescued for a final period of greatness by Augustin Amant Constant Fidel Edouart, who was born at Dunkirk in 1789, the sixteenth child of his parents (Plate LXVIII). This artist came to England in 1814 after fighting in the Napoleonic wars, for which service he had been decorated. He tried to earn his living by teaching French, but finding his efforts in this direction not very well patronized he took up the craft of making pictures in hair and wax. He carried this on for some time but later he found that he had a talent for taking profiles, and from then on he was able to give full rein to his hitherto unsuspected genius in this branch of portraiture. And what a genius it was! There are few profilists to equal Edouart, either in artistic quality or in profusion of output. It has been ascertained that he cut something like 100,000 profiles, almost every one of them of a consistently high quality of characterization. He cut all his profiles with scissors in black paper, and completely scorned all further decoration, in the form either of colour or of bronzing, returning with complete success to the simple classicism of the plain black shade and once again raising the art to the high standard of which it is capable when in the right hands. He travelled all over the British Isles, taking thousands upon thousands of portraits in profile, among them shades of such famous personages as Sir Walter Scott, the Bourbon Charles X, and his exiled court at Holyrood.

One of the most famous stories in the history of silhouettes centres around Edouart. In 1849 he decided to return home to France, and he sailed in November of that year, taking with him his enormous collection of duplicate shades, which were contained in several albums. The ship ran into storms almost as soon as it left port, and was finally wrecked on the rocks in Vazon Bay, Guernsey. In the wreck most of the duplicates (which, needless to say, would be priceless to-day) were lost. The remainder, some 12,000 in number, he presented to a family who had given him shelter after the wreck —these were purchased at a much later date by Mrs. Nevill Jackson, the famous collector.

Edouart did a certain amount of work after this time, but not on the prolific scale of his earlier years. He died at Guines in 1861, the last great name in profiles, and maybe the greatest freehand cutter that has ever been known. Moreover, he wrote a treatise on the art which ranks in importance with Nicholas Hilliard's treatise on miniature painting.

A personality of this last brilliant period was Master William James Hubard, a child prodigy, who was born in 1807. He was yet another freehand cutter, but his work, fine though it is in some respects, is not to be compared with that of Edouart. He certainly had great claims made for him as will be seen from the following advertisement, which appeared in a Norwich paper in January 1823—"Extraordinary Development of Juvenile Genius. Just arrived at Mr. Critchfield's, cutter, Market Place, Norwich. *Master Hubard*, The celebrated little artist who, by a mere glance at the face! and with a pair of common scissors!! not by the help of a Machine nor from any sketch with Pen, Pencil or Crayon, but from sight alone!!! cuts out the most spirited and striking likenesses in One Minute—Horses, Dogs, Carriages, in short every object in Nature and Art are the almost instantaneous productions of *His Talismanic Scissors*.

"Likenesses in Bust 1s. Two 1s. 6d./Young children 1s. 6d. Two 2s./ Full length 5s. Two 7s. 6d./Families attended at their houses; terms extra, if less than seven in number./Master H. may be seen from 11 in the morning until 4 and from 6 until 9 in the Evening."

Yet another advertisement tells us that Master Hubard was in 1823 presented with an expensive silver palette by the Glasgow Philosophical Society, and that by that Society his Exhibition was first designated the Hubard Gallery, which pretentious name he used for his headquarters where-ever he worked. Hubard also worked in America. His work is usually of the plain black and white variety, but he certainly used colour from time to time as well.

Amateurs flourished at this time, as well as at the earlier period of the art, and prominent amongst them was Mrs. Leigh Hunt, whose shade of Byron in riding costume was engraved in 1828 by Henry Golborn. Yet another amateur was the father of Lord Lister the surgeon, who cut his son's portrait when the latter was thirteen years of age.

THE RECENT HISTORY OF THE SILHOUETTE

With the invention of photography, silhouettes were bound to suffer the same fate as miniatures, and after the first half of the nineteenth century one hears very little of them; but the art was not entirely dead, for many artists have found a use for it, especially in book illustration, up to our own time.

Two such artists who come to mind at once in this connexion are Arthur Rackham and Claud Lovat Fraser. The former used it but rarely, but Fraser completely assimilated it and adapted it to his purposes. In his representations of theatrical scenes, and in his many decorative motifs designed for printing, this artist made full use of the shade's traditions.

The shade gives itself admirably to caricature and amongst those who have used it for this purpose from time to time are numbered Aubrey Beardsley, Phil May, Max Beerbohm, and H. M. Bateman. Phil May's silhouette caricatures are masterly, and deserve to be ranked with some of the art's finest achievements. Perhaps it is in caricature that the shade could most successfully be rehabilitated.

Although the shade's economic *raison d'être* came to an end with the invention of photography, that is no reason why the art should be allowed to die. It is a charming art, and although few profilists have been known in this country in recent years there seems no reason why its revival should not be effected as successfully as that of the miniature itself. Shades could be cut or painted for as little or less than it costs to have a photograph taken, and if properly executed could give in many cases a better likeness. That they can be cheap is amply demonstrated by the fact that one cutter named Handrup, who was working near Oxford Street in London until comparatively recently, would execute three portraits for 1s. 6d.! The writer has had no opportunity of examining this artist's work, but it was reputedly of a high standard. It was sometimes decorated with gold paint or chalk. In addition to portraits he also cut subject pieces in profile. Handrup was unfortunately killed in a motor accident in 1931, and quite apart from its personal consequences, his death was to be regretted as yet further depleting our already small number of silhouettists.

The work of H. Leslie, who worked before the war on the West Pier at Brighton, is of high quality—particularly in his subject work, which has great charm. In his designs for book-plates he demonstrated yet another application for the shade. That the public is still to be interested in the art was shown by his successful exhibition at 14 Brook Street in 1932. Queen Mary gave the art royal encouragement by purchasing one of his subject profiles, "Wisteria."

Finally there were Madie Roberts who worked in Hastings in 1918, producing profiles of R.A.F. Cadets; and S. M. Scott, A.R.M.S., who produced painted profiles, occasionally decorated with gold, and whose work was deemed worthy of acceptance by the Royal Hibernian Academy.

Frankly the art's future does not seem so assured as that of the miniature itself; but of course one cannot tell what coming years hold in store. Whilst the number of contemporary miniaturists is comparatively large, there are but few silhouettists at work, and many more will be required to assure a propitious future to the art. Compared with true miniature painting it is not a difficult art and is one which amateurs might practise with success; in fact the amateur with his limited time would be better advised to launch out upon such an art than on one that is so admittedly difficult as miniature painting. Many excellent profilists in the past have been amateurs—Major André is an obvious example—and when one remembers the hosts of amateurs in the reign of George III there seems no reason why modern people should not be equally successful. Both cutting and painting are comparatively easy techniques in making silhouettes, according to the abilities of the individual. It is in this direction that I feel the art has its greatest hope of survival, not as a rival to the professional photographer, for it has not the obvious advantages of the miniature to rival that formidable foe, but as a pastime in which the amateur may record the shades of his friends and loved ones in an intimate atmosphere by a homely fireside.

CHAPTER EIGHT

The Collector

FINALLY we come to that most important person, the collector. It is not within my province to justify collecting; I am a collector myself and the only justification that I would put forward for my urge is that I like to surround my everyday life with fine things—that in itself should suffice for any collector.

The collecting urge begins, as a rule, at an early age, usually being directed towards the acquisition of stamps, coins, matchboxes, and a hundred other kinds of bric-à-brac or curios. Later, if it persists, it assumes a more refined note; stamp-collecting becomes philately, coin-collecting becomes numismatics, the collector of cigarette-cards or matchbox-lids perhaps becomes a connoisseur of prints, paintings, or miniatures. The quest for the rare or beautiful may begin, however, at any age, and it is not uncommon for adults of quite advanced years suddenly to find that they have a love for china, for glass, for furniture, or for any of the hundred other branches of collecting.

Collectors of miniatures are divisible into two main groups; those who collect them with the object of building up a connoisseur's collection, which type we will call the specialist; and those who collect miniatures amongst other objects of art and virtu, or who make a special collection of miniatures on a small scale; this type falls into the category of the general collector. The second group is by far the larger, and embraces those who merely buy a miniature from time to time as a decoration for the walls of their homes, to those who collect with some real knowledge of the subject, but without the specialist's wider knowledge and experience. It is to collectors of this group, together with those who wish to begin a more specialized collection that this chapter is addressed. The experienced connoisseur will require no help from me, for his own expert knowledge, supplemented by the learned specialist treatises, will range far beyond the limits of this modest introduction to the subject.

8—(D.107)

I recommend that before the intending collector makes any purchases at all he should spend as much time as possible in museums and picture galleries where miniatures are displayed. Study all the examples you can, both in these places and anywhere else where they are to be found. Never miss an opportunity of looking closely at any miniature of any period. Take note of the colours used by individual artists, and the way in which their paint is applied. Study what materials were in use at particular periods (for example no miniatures were painted on ivory until the seventeenth century), and what general stylistic changes took place as one period gave way to another. In this way you will acquire a practical and critical foundation for your future activities that will be of unlimited benefit to you in years to come. Remember that if the collector is to collect intelligently he needs training and experience quite as much as the painter himself. Lack of knowledge leads to the acquisition of forgeries and other rubbish that will destroy the pleasure of collecting altogether.

BUYING MINIATURES

When you are ready to buy it is far better, and also cheaper in the long run, to buy your miniatures from reputable sources. By that I do not necessarily mean the most famous dealers. There are many good small shops with but a local reputation which from time to time offer excellent miniatures at the most reasonable prices. I have bought good examples of Persian miniatures for as little as a few shillings apiece from such dealers, and English miniatures by good artists for a little more. On one occasion I was lucky enough to buy a delightful little monochrone miniature of a girl playing ball, by Lord Leighton, P.R.A., executed in pink water-colour, for as little as half a guinea! And this was not a "find"—the dealer knew very well what it was and pointed it out to me as such. Of course you could not expect to buy a Hilliard or a Cooper for such a sum, but even so, for the more affluent collector, miniatures by such artists may sometimes be bought for as little as £100 each—a small sum indeed when one thinks of the prices paid for large paintings by many lesser artists. The larger dealers, too, are always ready to help, and often enough their wares are far from overpriced; also one has the added advantage of expert advice from such a source. The same applies to the large firms of auctioneers, who carefully scrutinize their lots before putting them up for sale. "Discoveries" of good work in junk-shops, pawnbrokers' shops, and elsewhere are but a rare occurrence, and it is not wise to wait for such a happening. By all means sort through anything that may be offered for sale in such places, but be on your guard, for some of these dealers are a great deal more knowledgeable than they appear to be, and a fine-looking miniature offered at a knock-out price should be viewed with every suspicion. Is it a copy? Is it a cleverly faked print? If you are satisfied that it is what it appears to be, then buy it by all means—you can never be absolutely certain until you have got it away and examined it out of its frame with the most searching exactitude, and if it appears to be reasonably priced, then the risk is worth taking. You are sure to have some disappointments, though it is as well to guard against them as much as possible. In the long run, however, the reputable dealer, large or small, is the best source of supply. Ninety-nine times out of a hundred, if a work turns out to be other than what he represented it to be, such a dealer will take it back and refund your money.

CARE OF MINIATURES

When you have acquired a few specimens, the next thing to decide is how to keep them. Some people like to place them on their walls in groups, or to fill up odd spaces in corners, above doors, or in other similar places. There is no doubt that this is the best way in which to place your specimens in order to derive the greatest possible pleasure from them. In time they become a part of your life; a face becomes an old friend, and some scene from the past provides a window looking out into another age. Some collectors prefer to wrap up their miniatures in tissue-paper and keep them in a drawer or a cabinet, but although such a method certainly gives every protection the miniatures do not have a fair chance to enter into the life of their owner. They remain museum-pieces and their delightful sparkle is left to languish sadly behind a stifling muffler of wrappings. Even museums do not usually go to such lengths, but are content to house their miniatures in glass cases with a curtain covering which can be drawn aside and replaced. If you decide to keep your works in a cabinet this is by far the best method, although it is really only necessary to cover the miniatures when the days are bright. If you acquire many specimens over the course of a few years, it is a good idea to keep some in a cabinet and to change those on your walls from time to time. This is ideal and besides giving the miniatures themselves a rest from the light and atmosphere it keeps your own interest in them completely alert. With a constant change you will never tire of them.

Wherever you house your miniatures, make sure that they are not in direct sunlight. No miniature can stand that, even if painted in the most permanent colours. The carnations, as the cheek tints are called, are especially liable to fade. Neither should they be put on a damp wall, nor in a room that is not often used. This will inevitably cause mildew to form inside the frame—one of the commonest curses of the miniature-collector's life. If this happens do not attempt to clean it yourself but leave it to an expert, who is far less likely to cause damage. Yet another thing to guard against, especially in the case of miniatures painted on ivory, is too much warmth, such as is usually encountered on a wall immediately above a fire. This will often cause the ivory to crack, which will put the miniature beyond human aid. Moreover, if the miniature is placed above a fireplace, smoke is liable to get into the frame and discolour the paint. If these few simple rules are borne in mind, however, there is little to fear. Exercise a little common sense in placing them and in their subsequent care, and you will have little cause for apprehension about their safety. Enamels, I need hardly add, are much more hardy, and so long as they are not dropped will stand up to almost any conditions so far as warmth, light, and atmosphere are concerned.

IDENTIFYING ARTIST AND SUBJECT

Naturally, you will want to learn all you can about your miniatures. You can often find interesting information written on their backs, or on scraps of paper hidden behind them in their frames. Quite a number of miniaturists only signed their work on the back—Cosway rarely signed on the front— and there is always a chance that a hitherto unidentified miniature will yield up the name of its creator when it is removed from its frame for inspection. More often than not you will find no more than a few scraps of paper, but even these may be of use to some future expert into whose hands the miniature may fall, so be very careful to replace everything that you have removed. It is impossible for even the most knowledgeable expert to identify every miniature, so do not be disappointed if you are not successful in every case. After all, you still have the work itself which is the most important thing, and its very enigma will add to its fascination. It is often easier to identify a sitter in a miniature than to identify its creator. Sometimes their names are labelled behind or on a scrap of paper inside, and in the case of some portraits, the name, or initials, and age of the sitter are written on the front. Also, if the sitter was a person of rank, there may exist other portraits in other forms, such as oils, engravings, and pastels, with which comparisons may be made. With both the artist and his subjects, however, make absolutely sure that your conclusions are correct before labelling your specimens. This will ensure that no subsequent collector will be misled by false or uncertain conclusions. When you have satisfied yourself regarding your attributions, get them checked by an expert, to make doubly sure that you are right.

ILLUMINATIONS

If you decide to collect illuminations, your scope will be much more limited than with framed miniatures. Initials and miniatures, clipped from old illuminations by some vandal's hand, are common enough, it is true, and from a comparative point of view form an excellent basis for any collection. Suitably framed, with a mount to prevent them from touching the glass and thus avoiding any damage to the gold by contact with any condensation that may form on its surface, they are decorative and colourful. But the larger field of illuminated books belongs to the wealthy expert, and the greatest number that any average collector could hope to acquire could be counted on the fingers of one hand.

These few remarks should, I feel, suffice for the beginner or for the smaller collector. For those who require fuller knowledge I recommend one of the small handbooks mentioned in the bibliography, which will prove a useful stepping-stone from the novice's to the specialist's knowledge.

However far you go with your collector's urge you will find that miniatures are amongst the most fascinating objects in the world and that they will repay your attention more than any other form of painting will.

BIBLIOGRAPHY

THE bibliography of miniature painting is a very large one, and ranges from small handbooks and monographs, written from a general angle, to sumptuous *éditions de luxe* dealing with individual painters and their work. The following selection is intended as a cross-section of the available literature, and does not pretend to be exhaustive. Most of the books are out of print, as few books have been written on the subject in recent years, but many of them are easily obtainable at varying prices from good booksellers.

Of the authors mentioned, special mention must be made of the late Dr. George Charles Williamson, who until his death was librarian of the Royal Society of Miniature Painters. This collector devoted the greater part of his life to the subject of the portrait miniature, and amassed an enormous knowledge on the subject. His facts are quite reliable, but from time to time his opinions incline to be rather dogmatic. The reader should bear this in mind and should not be afraid to form his own opinions as to the merits or demerits of the work of various miniaturists throughout the art's history. Do not misunderstand me; I am not decrying Williamson's work, but merely warning the beginner to beware of a great man's dogmas.

The late J. J. Foster, an enthusiastic amateur, also deserves special mention for his valuable work; likewise the late Dr. Lumsden Propert, a great pioneer to whose spade-work we owe so much of our present knowledge on the subject.

CHAMBERLAIN, ARTHUR B.
Hans Holbein the Younger (1913)
A standard work on this artist. Well written with copious annotations. Good illustrations.

CHRISTIE, MANSON, AND WOODS
This firm issues catalogues of sales (many of which are illustrated). Advertised in *The Times* on Tuesdays. Of great value to the collector and student.

COKE, DESMOND

The Art of Silhouette (1913)

A small handbook, written from an appreciative angle.

FOSTER, J. J.

Miniature Painters, British and Foreign (1903, 2 vols.)

A lavishly illustrated *édition-de-luxe*.

Chats on Old Miniatures (1908)

A small general handbook, of great value to the beginner. Illustrated.

Samuel Cooper (1914)

The standard treatise on this miniaturist. Beautifully illustrated. Rare; edition was limited to 150 copies.

Dictionary of Painters of Miniatures (1921)

Excellent work of reference.

GIBSON, W. P.

Wallace Collection Catalogues: Miniatures and Illuminations (1935)

Important as a work of reference. Contains biographical information regarding artists and sitters. Well illustrated.

HARRISON, F.

English Manuscripts of the 14th Century (1937)

A very good book, illustrated by colour plates.

HILLIARD, NICHOLAS

A Treatise Concerning the Arte of Limning (1912, Vol. 1 of Walpole Society)

The most important document on technique in the history of the portrait miniature. Introduction and notes by Philip Norman, LL.D. Should be in the possession of all who are interested in the art.

JACKSON, MRS. NEVILL

Silhouette (1938)

Lavishly illustrated and well written. Contains an exhaustive dictionary of silhouettists with copious biographical information. A first-class work.

The History of Silhouettes (1911)

Ancestors in Silhouette by August Edouart (1920)

JAMES, M. R.

A Descriptive Catalogue of the Manuscripts in the Fitzwilliam Museum (1895)
An important catalogue and an authoritative work of reference. Illustrated with photogravure plates.

KENDRICK, T. D.

Anglo-Saxon Art to A.D. 900
A first-class work. Pays special attention to the decorative *motifs* of Anglo-Saxon mss. and their sources. Well illustrated.

LESLIE, HUBERT

Silhouettes and Scissor Cutting (1939)
A book of instruction; of especial interest to the amateur or beginner.

LONG, BASIL S.

Catalogue of the Jones Collection. Part III. Paintings and Miniatures (1923)
Published by the Victoria and Albert Museum, this is important as a smaller work of reference. Contains much useful biographical information on artists and sitters. Illustrated.

British Miniaturists, 1520–1860 (1929)

MIDDLETON, J. HENRY

Illuminated Manuscripts in Classical and Mediaeval Times (1892)
An excellent work of reference and highly readable. Illustrations are not good by present standards, but the letterpress is excellent.

MILLENET, LOUIS-ELIE

Enamelling on Metal. Translated by H. de Koningh (1947)
This small book gives detailed instructions on the practice of the art. Authoritative and of great interest.

NORGATE, EDWARD

Miniatura or the Art of Limning. Edited by Martin Hardie (1919).
Modern edition of an old treatise on Technique written c. 1650.

PEACHAM, HENRY

The Gentleman's Exercise (1634)
An old treatise on Technique; valuable to both artist and collector.

POPE-HENNESSY, JOHN

A Lecture on Nicholas Hilliard (1949).
A well-illustrated and interesting title work on this miniaturist.

PROPERT, J. LUMSDEN

History of Miniature Art (1887)
One of the earliest books on the subject. Much of its content is out of
date, but still a book of importance as a pioneer work.

SOTHEBY AND CO.

See note after Christie, Manson, and Woods.

VICTORIA AND ALBERT MUSEUM

This museum has published many catalogues and pamphlets on the
subject. Information regarding them is sent on receipt of a stamp to
defray postage. "A Guide to the Salting Collection" may be specially
noted.

VON BOEHN, MAX

Miniatures and Silhouettes. Translated by E. V. Walker (1928)
A well-illustrated and pleasing little handbook. Deals with the sitters
more than the artists concerned. Deals particularly with foreign
miniatures.

WALPOLE, HORACE

Anecdotes of Painters in England (various editions)
A good work of reference, but the reader should remember that Walpole
could be very prejudiced.

BIBLIOGRAPHY

WILLIAMSON, G. C.

Richard Cosway, R.A. (1897, and, in smaller form, 1905)
The standard work on this artist. Well illustrated.

George Engleheart, 1752–1829 (1902)
The standard work on this artist. Well illustrated.

Andrew and Nathaniel Plimer (1903)
The standard work on these artists. Well illustrated.

Ozias Humphry, R.A., 1743–1808 (1919)
The standard work on this artist. Well illustrated.

John Zoffany, R.A. (1920)
The standard work on this artist. Well illustrated.

How to Identify Portrait Miniatures (1904)
A good small handbook, with chapters on technique by Alyn Williams, P.R.M.S. Illustrated.

The Miniature Collector (1921)
Written to replace the aforementioned. Illustrated. Perhaps the most useful small handbook on the subject.

Catalogue of the Collection of Miniatures, the Property of the late Mr. J. Pierpont Morgan. 4 vols. (1906–7)
The most lavish catalogue on the subject ever made. Far beyond the reach of the average pocket, but mentioned here in view of its unique character. Very richly illustrated by photogravure plates, many of which are hand-coloured. Copies are in several museums and can usually be consulted by bona fide students upon application.

Portrait Miniatures, English and Foreign (1910)
A book, primarily of importance on account of its good illustrations; short introductory essay.

The Art of the Miniature Painter (1926)
A book mainly of interest on account of its treatise on technique contributed by Percy Buckman, R.M.S.

WINTER, CARL

Elizabethan Miniatures (1943)

A really delightful little book in the King Penguin series. Illustrated by colour plates.

In addition to the above, many art magazines publish articles on the subject from time to time, and also give lists of prices realized at sales, with market comments.

INDEX

The Subject Miniature

PLATE IX

THE BOOK OF DURROW

Trinity College, Dublin.

PLATE X

$13\frac{1}{2} \times 9\frac{3}{4}$ *in.*

THE LINDISFARNE GOSPELS

B.M.f.26b.

PLATE XI

12 × 9 in.

THE ST. CHAD'S GOSPELS
Lichfield Cathedral, f.218.

PLATE XII

THE CANTERBURY PSALTER
B.M. f.30b, M.S. Vespas, A.1.

PLATE XIII

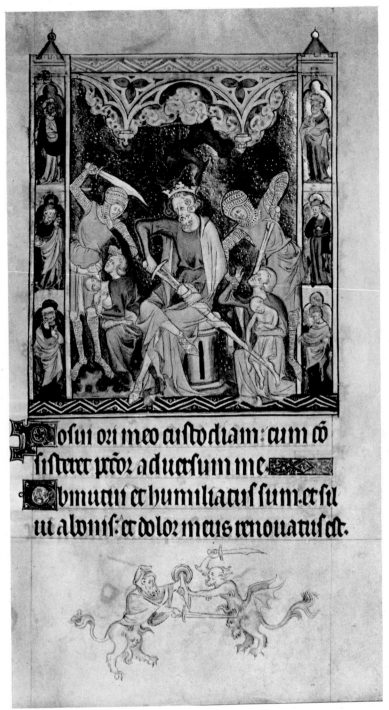

10¾ × 7 in.

QUEEN MARY'S PSALTER

B.M. f.132 R, Royal MS. 2 B. vii.

PLATE XIV

BIBLIA SACRA (Anglo-Norman)
Fitzwilliam Museum, No. 43.
MS. 2 in James catalogue.

PLATE XV

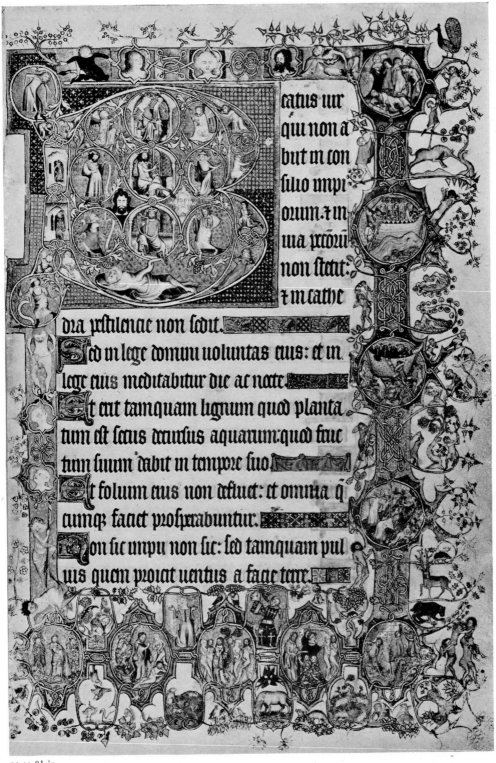

13 × 8½ in.

THE ST. OMER PSALTER

B.M. f.7 R, Add. MS. 39810.

PLATE XVI

HORAE (Fifteenth-century English)

Fitzwilliam Museum, No. 46.
MS. 57 in James catalogue.

PLATE XVII

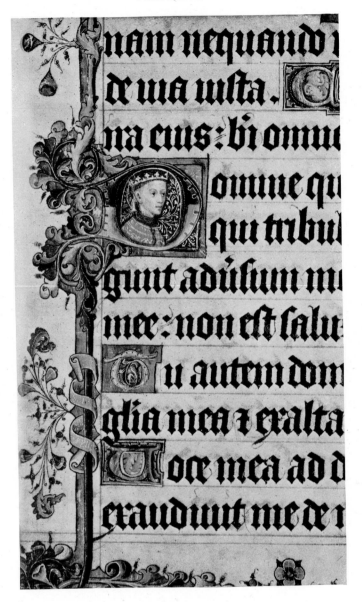

THE BOOK OF HOURS OF JOHN,
DUKE OF BEDFORD
B.M. f.74 A

PLATE XVIII

Enamel

WILLIAM BIRCH

Landscape with Women Bathing

Victoria & Albert Museum, P.14–1920.
Crown copyright.

PLATE XIX

$10\frac{1}{4} \times 7\frac{13}{16}$ *in.*

BERNARD LENS

Landscape with River and Figures (After Vandervaart)

Victoria & Albert Museum, P.1–1934.
Crown copyright.

PLATE XX

Enamel

WILLIAM ESSEX

Flowers (After Nicolaes van Veerendael)

Victoria & Albert Museum, 930–1868.
Crown copyright.

PLATE XXI

Enamel. 7 × 8½ *in.*

WILLIAM ESSEX

Cupid Disarmed by a Nymph (After William Hilton, R.A.)

Victoria & Albert Museum, 924–1868.
Crown copyright.

PLATE XXII

PETER PAUL LENS
A Ragged Boy
Victoria & Albert Museum, P.8–1920.
Crown copyright.

PLATE XXIII

7½ × 5¼ in.

ALFRED TIDEY

White Mice

Victoria & Albert Museum, P.85–1935.
Crown copyright.

PLATE XXIV

JAMES SCOULER

Diana

Victoria & Albert Museum, P.78–1928.
Crown copyright.

The Portrait Miniature

PLATE XXV

HANS HOLBEIN THE YOUNGER
The Princess Anne of Cleves
*Victoria & Albert Museum, P.153–1910.
Crown copyright.*

HANS HOLBEIN THE YOUNGER
Portrait of the Artist
(Painted on a playing-card)
Wallace Collection, M.203, by permission.

PLATE XXVI

$2\frac{3}{8} \times 1\frac{7}{8}$ in.

NICHOLAS HILLIARD
Unknown Man, 1572
Victoria & Albert Museum, P.1–1942.
Crown copyright.

NICHOLAS HILLIARD
Queen Elizabeth
Victoria & Albert Museum, 4404–1857.
Crown copyright.

NICHOLAS HILLIARD
Queen Elizabeth
Victoria & Albert Museum, 622–1882.
Crown copyright.

PLATE XXVII

10⅛ × 7 *in.*

NICHOLAS HILLIARD
George Clifford, Earl of Cumberland
National Maritime Museum, Greenwich.

PLATE XXVIII

NICHOLAS HILLIARD

An Unknown Youth Leaning against a Tree among Roses

Victoria & Albert Museum, P.163–1910.
Crown copyright.

PLATE XXIX

ISAAC OLIVER

Portrait of a Young Man said to be
Sir Philip Sidney

Collection of H.M. The King at Windsor Castle
By gracious permission of H.M. The King.

PLATE XXX

LAURENCE HILLIARD
Lady in a Black Hat
*Victoria & Albert Museum transferred from
the British Museum. Crown copyright.*

ISAAC OLIVER
Henry Frederick, Prince of Wales
Fitzwilliam Museum.

ISAAC OLIVER
Lady in Masque Costume
*Victoria & Albert Museum, P.3–1942.
Crown copyright.*

PLATE XXXI

9¼ × 6 in.

ISAAC OLIVER
Richard Sackville, Earl of Dorset
Victoria & Albert Museum, 721–1882.
Crown copyright.

PLATE XXXII

ISAAC OLIVER

Called "Lucy Harington, Countess of Bedford"

Fitzwilliam Museum.

PLATE XXXIII

PETER OLIVER
Sir Francis Nethersole
Victoria & Albert Museum, 6–1917
Crown copyright.

JOHN HOSKINS
Queen Henrietta Maria
Fitzwilliam Museum.

SAMUEL COOPER
A Gentleman, Possibly Sir R. Henley,
Formerly called a Portrait of Edward
Montagu, First Earl of Sandwich
Victoria & Albert Museum, P.113–1910.
Crown copyright.

PLATE XXXIV

THOMAS FLATMAN

Self-Portrait

Victoria & Albert Museum, P.79–1938.
Crown copyright.

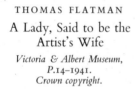

$2\frac{3}{4} \times 2\frac{3}{16}$ *in.*

THOMAS FLATMAN

A Lady, Said to be the
Artist's Wife

Victoria & Albert Museum,
P.14–1941.
Crown copyright.

PLATE XXXV

$1\frac{1}{16} \times 1\ in.$

SAMUEL COOPER

Charles II, when Young

Victoria & Albert Museum, Jones Collection No. 597.
Crown copyright.

$3\frac{1}{8} \times 2\frac{1}{2}\ in.$

THOMAS FLATMAN

Charles II (After a portrait by Lely,
engraved by A. Blooteling, 1680)

From the original in the Wallace Collection, M.109,
by permission.

PLATE XXXVI

NICHOLAS DIXON

General Charles Churchill, Brother
of the Duke of Marlborough

Victoria & Albert Museum, P.124–1910.
Crown copyright.

NATHANIEL PLIMER

Mr. Alexander Sprot or Dr.
Adam Sprott of Edinburgh

Victoria & Albert Museum, P.101–1910.
Crown copyright.

$3\frac{3}{32} \times 2\frac{9}{16}$ *in.*

LAURENCE CROSSE

Supposed Portrait of one of the Barons Maynard

Victoria & Albert Museum, P.106–1910.
Crown copyright.

PLATE XXXVII

JOHN SMART
A Girl in White
From the original in the Wallace Collection,
M.308, by permission.

JOHN SMART
An Unknown Lady, 1779
Victoria & Albert Museum, P.10–1929.
Crown copyright.

JOHN SMART
Self-Portrait
Victoria & Albert Museum, P.11–1940.
Crown copyright.

$3\frac{13}{32} \times 2\frac{23}{32}$ *in.*

PLATE XXXVIII

ANDREW PLIMER
Sir Christopher Pegge, M.D., F.R.S.,
at Oxford

Victoria & Albert Museum, P.91–1910.
Crown copyright.

$2\frac{5}{8} \times 2\frac{1}{8}$ *in.*

ANDREW PLIMER
A Gentleman
Victoria & Albert Museum, P.29–1910.
Crown copyright.

RICHARD COSWAY, R.A.
A Gentleman
Victoria & Albert Museum, P.46–1910.
Crown copyright.

$3\frac{15}{32} \times 2\frac{7}{8}$ *in.*

PLATE XXXIX

RICHARD COSWAY, R.A.

Maria, Daughter of W. Smythe,
afterwards Mrs. Fitzherbert

*From the original in the Wallace Collection, M.87.
by permission.*

RICHARD COSWAY, R.A.

Miss Crofton

*From the original in the Wallace Collection, M.88,
by permission.*

PLATE XL

GEORGE ENGLEHEART
Mr. John Dyer Collier
Victoria & Albert Museum, P.76–1910.
Crown copyright.

GEORGE ENGLEHEART
Charlotte-Augusta, Princess Royal,
Daughter of George III
From the original in the Wallace Collection, M.103,
by permission.

PLATE XLI

GEORGE ENGLEHEART
An Unknown Lady, 1780
Victoria & Albert Museum, P.75–1931.
Crown copyright.

PLATE XLII

JOHN LINNELL
An Unknown Man
Victoria & Albert Museum, P.11–1937.
Crown copyright.

J. C. D. ENGLEHEART
A Girl, Said to be Miss Mary Engleheart
Victoria & Albert Museum, P.10–1944.
Crown copyright.

PLATE XLIII

9⅜ × 5⁵⁄₁₆ *in.*

SIMON JACQUES ROCHARD
Miss and Master Stirling
Victoria & Albert Museum, P.106–1931.
Crown copyright.

PLATE XLIV

5¼ × 3¹¹⁄₁₆ in.

SIR W. C. ROSS, R.A.

Harriet, Countess Gower, Afterward Duchess of Sutherland

From the original in the Wallace Collection, M.290,
by permission.

*The Contemporary School
of Miniature Painters*

PLATE XLV

LISA DE MONTFORT, R.M.S.
Meum Stewart

LISA DE MONTFORT, R.M.S.
John Pemberton

PLATE XLVI

MARJORY FORBES, R.M.S.
Bridget

MARJORY FORBES, R.M.S.
Sheila Ann Mackinnon

PLATE XLVII

HOPE DOUGLAS, R.M.S.
Hope Helen

LISA DE MONTFORT, R.M.S.
Etienne Amyot

PLATE XLVIII

JOAN AYLING, R.M.S.
Eleonore in Fancy Dress

PLATE XLIX

JOAN AYLING, R.M.S.

Rai

JOAN AYLING, R.M.S.

Ann

PLATE L

I. C. MONCRIEFF–BELL
Miss Jenkin

KATHLEEN GOODMAN
Indian Prince

PLATE LI

$3\frac{1}{4} \times 2\frac{3}{4}$ in.

KATHLEEN MAUDE, A.R.M.S.

The Snore

PLATE LII

G. LONDON WOOD

A Somerset Rockery

PLATE LIII

LT.-COL. F. A. GODDARD, O.B.E., R.M.S.
The Old Life-boat Slip at Selsey

PLATE LIV

Painted on opal glass

DAYSI M. BROOKES, A.R.M.S.

Costume Piece

$3\frac{1}{8} \times 4$ *in.*

ISABEL SAUL, R.M.S., F.R.S.A.

Mrs. Saul

PLATE LV

ALICE BINGHAM
Flowers

$3\frac{1}{2} \times 2\frac{1}{2}$ *in.*

MARJORIE RODGERS, R.M.S.
Tulips

PLATE LVI

After which usually follows

THE LITANY OF THE

BLESSED VIRGIN.

Kyrie eleison,
Kyrie eleison,
Christi eleison,
Christi eleison,
Kyrie eleison,
Kyrie eleison,
Christi exaudi nos,
Christi exaudi nos,
Pater de cælis Deus,
Miserere nobis
Fili Redemptor mundi,
    Deus,
Miserere nobis,
Spiritus Sancte Deus,
Miserere nobis
Sancta Trinitas unus Deus,
Miserere nobis

Size of each page 5⅝ × 4 *in.*

ALBERT COUSINS, HON. R.M.S.

Double-page Opening from an Illuminated Benedictional
In the Author's Collection.

PLATE LVII

15 × 13½ in.

ISABEL SAUL, R.M.S., F.R.S.A.
City of Canterbury

PLATE LVIII

ROSEMARY SUTCLIFF, A.R.M.S.
White Horses

PLATE LIX

MARJORIE RODGERS, R.M.S.
Masquerade

PLATE LX

JOYCE KILBURN, R.M.S.
On the Stairs

The Silhouette

PLATE LXI

A. CHARLES
A Gentleman
Victoria & Albert Museum, P.137–1922.
Crown copyright.

On glass; $3\frac{5}{16} \times 2\frac{11}{16}$ in.

MRS. ISABELLA BEETHAM
Mrs. Lloyd Jones (Née Bridgett Lloyd)
Victoria & Albert Museum.
Crown copyright.

PLATE LXII

Attributed to SAMUEL COTES
Alleged Portrait of Major John André
Victoria & Albert Museum, 340–1903
Crown copyright.

T. HAMLET
Elizabeth Anne Tydell
Victoria & Albert Museum, P.132–1923.
Crown copyright.

On glass.

PLATE LXIII

PORTRAIT OF A GENTLEMAN.
DRAWN IN° NOVEMBER 1836, BY FOSTER: POSSIBLY BY
b.1762]   EDWARD WARD FOSTER   [d.1865.
N° P.13-1927.

On card 4$\frac{9}{16}$ × 3$\frac{1}{2}$ in.

Perhaps by EDWARD WARD FOSTER
A Gentleman, Profile
Victoria & Albert Museum P.13-1927.
Crown copyright.

PLATE LXIV

$4\frac{7}{32} \times 3\frac{1}{4}$ in.

Perhaps by J. BUNCOMBE
An Officer of the 97th Foot Regiment

Victoria & Albert Museum, P.127–1922.
Crown copyright.

PLATE LXV

$3\frac{7}{8} \times 3\frac{3}{8}$ in.

Perhaps by J. BUNCOMBE
An Officer of the 89th Foot Regiment

Victoria & Albert Museum, P.126–1922.
Crown copyright.

PLATE LXVI

MRS. SARAH HARRINGTON
Anna Maria, Third Duchess of Newcastle
Victoria & Albert Museum, P.161–1922.
Crown copyright.

Cut in white paper and placed over black

RAYMOND LISTER, R.M.S., F.R.S.A.
Portrait of the Artist's Wife

PLATE LXVII

On glass; $4\frac{13}{32} \times 3\frac{19}{32}$ *in.*

N. SPORNBERG

The Rev. Abraham Kirkpatrick Sherson

Victoria & Albert Museum, P.83–1920.
Crown copyright.

PLATE LXVIII

Major Brereton — taken from description, died 127 years ago.
Bath 23d May 1827 —

7¾ × 7¼ in.

A. EDOUART
Major Brereton
Victoria & Albert Museum, E.2423–1913.
Crown copyright.